Flannery O'Connor and the Church Made Visible

RALPH C. WOOD

Flannery O'Connor and the Church Made Visible

A Revolutionary Witness for the Sake of the Gospel

BAYLOR UNIVERSITY PRESS

Cover and Book Design by Elyxandra Encarnación
Cover image: Flannery O'Connor, self-portrait, courtesy of the Mary Flannery O'Connor Charitable Trust

The Library of Congress has cataloged this book under ISBN 978-1-4813-2187-7.

Library of Congress Control Number: 2024940027

CONTENTS

Introduction

> The Church is the visible form of Christ in the world. The Church is the presence of Christ in the same way that Christ is the presence of God.
>
> **Dietrich Bonhoeffer**

During the two decades following the publication of *Flannery O'Connor and the Christ-Haunted South* (Eerdmans, 2004), I have continued my career-long devotion to O'Connor by publishing a dozen more essays on her life and work. Here I have gathered eight of them, all radically revised, so as to make them freshly available.[1] Fifteen years ago Stanley Hauerwas and I argued that, despite Chesterton's celebrated claim that America is a nation with the soul of a church, the Church as the visible form of Christ had become virtually invisible. Our argument still holds, and it thus forms the opening chapter of this book. It is not a complaint against secularization. Rather is it a call to make the Church visible by offering its ever-old, ever-new Gospel in compelling literary ways. As I will seek to show, Flannery O'Connor is our strongest exemplar of this salutary mission.[2]

1 Chapters 3 and 9 are new and, I believe, much needed.

2 All O'Connor quotations are taken from these editions of her work and will be paginated within the text:

Flannery O'Connor Collected Works, ed. Sally Fitzgerald (New York: Library of America, 1988). CW

The Habit of Being: Letters, ed. and intro. Sally Fitzgerald (New York: Farrar, Straus & Giroux, 1979). HB

Mystery and Manners: Occasional Prose, sel. and ed. Sally and Robert Fitzgerald (New York: Farrar, Straus & Giroux, 1962). MM

Benedict XVI on Christians as a Permanent Minority

This is not a time for casting Christian stones to smash the brittle glass of our idolatrous culture.[3] Our churches have been so thoroughly embedded in our regnant social, political, and economic assumptions that they cannot claim to be "in the world but not of the world."[4] We have brought our calamity on ourselves. Henri de Lubac was right to observe in 1947 that the French Revolution would never have occurred—or at least that its Reign of Terror would not have been so violent—if the Catholic Church had not so thoroughly allied itself with the French nation-state.[5]

No one has discerned this ecclesial failure more acutely than the late Emeritus Pope Benedict XVI. Already in 1969 Cardinal Ratzinger was confessing the long-term results of this colossal failure. It means that Christians must come to grips with our new status as a permanent minority:

[3] I generally avoid the word "secular" because our age has not witnessed the eclipse of the true God so much as the proliferation of idols: nationalism, militarism, consumerism, hedonism, etc. St. Paul would have recognized them now as in first-century Athens: "I see that in every way you are very religious" (Acts 17:22, NIV).
Neither is it correct to regard our culture as pagan:

> In theological terms, pagans are oriented toward the immanent. The pagan gods, in all their beauty and terror, are elements *of this world*, in contrast to the transcendent God of the Abrahamic faiths. To be sure, Christianity incorporated immanent elements over time. The ancient sacralization of sites such as wells and stones persisted, but with heathen deities replaced by Christian hermits or martyrs. Pagan festivals became entwined with the Christian calendar. The pantheon of deities was replaced by an ever-growing host of saints. Christianity flourished when it permitted followers to incorporate religious practices that were found, not only in Greek and Roman religion, but in many other religions—practices that seem, in fact, to be instinctive in human beings, particularly the veneration of nature and of ancestors.

Louise Perry, "We Are Repaganizing," *First Things*, https://www.firstthings.com/article/2023/10/we-are-repaganizing (emphasis original).

[4] This summons is voiced most scandalously in John 15:18–19 (ESV): "If the world hates you, know that it has hated me before it hated you. If you were of the world, the world would love you as its own; but because you are not of the world, but I chose you out of the world, therefore the world hates you."

[5] Henri de Lubac, *Catholicism: Christ and the Common Destiny of Man*, trans. Lancelot C. Sheppard and Sister Elizabeth Englund, OCD (San Francisco: Ignatius Press, 1988).

> From the crisis of today the Church of tomorrow will emerge—a Church that has lost much. She will become small and will have to start afresh more or less from the beginning. She will no longer be able to inhabit many of the edifices she built in prosperity. As the number of her adherents diminishes, so it will lose many of her social privileges. In contrast to an earlier age, it will be seen much more as a voluntary society, entered only by free decision. As a small society, it will make much bigger demands on the initiative of her individual members. Undoubtedly it will discover new forms of ministry and will ordain to the priesthood approved Christians who pursue some profession. In many smaller congregations or in self-contained social groups, pastoral care will normally be provided in this fashion. Along-side this, the full-time ministry of the priesthood will be indispensable as formerly. But in all of the changes at which one might guess, the Church will find her essence afresh and with full conviction in that which was always at her center: faith in the triune God, in Jesus Christ, the Son of God made man, in the presence of the Spirit until the end of the world. In faith and prayer she will again recognize the sacraments as the worship of God and not as a subject for liturgical scholarship.

Such down-sizing modesty will require ecclesial disentanglement from all forms of hegemonic power, whether religious or secular:

> The Church will be a more spiritual Church, not presuming upon a political mandate, flirting as little with the Left as with the Right. It will be hard going for the Church, for the process of crystallization and clarification will cost her much valuable energy. It will make her poor and cause her to become the Church of the meek. The process will be all the more arduous, for sectarian narrow-mindedness as well as pompous self-will will have to be shed. One may predict that all of this will take time. The process will be long and wearisome. . . . But when the trial of this sifting is past, a great power will flow from a more spiritualized and simplified Church. Men in a totally planned world will find themselves unspeakably lonely. If they have completely lost sight of God, they will feel the whole horror of their poverty. Then they will discover the little flock of believers as something wholly new. They will discover it as a hope that is meant for them, an answer for which they have always been searching in secret.

Far from prompting despair, this long twilight struggle will be invigorated by radical hope:

> And so it seems certain to me that the Church is facing very hard times. The real crisis has scarcely begun. We will have to count on terrific upheavals. But I am equally certain about what will remain at the end: not the Church of the political cult, which is dead already, but the Church of faith. It may well no longer be the dominant social power to the extent that she was until recently; but it will enjoy a fresh blossoming and be seen as man's home, where he will find life and hope beyond death.[6]

This Benedictine summons is not a call for our churches to regard their chief mission as the revival of our moribund culture. Such partial restoration may be its salutary side effect, but our chief mission must be the renewal of the witness of our churches. In their leanness and loneliness—paradoxically strong in being weak and marginalized—we who are their members must also uphold the work of writers whose literary vision accords with the Gospel, especially when testing and challenging rather than easily confirming it.

Dietrich Bonhoeffer on the Non-Competitive Church

Dietrich Bonhoeffer offers a Protestant parallel to the Benedictine way forward. He speaks of "Christ existing as community." By this he does not mean that the public Church can be identified with the presence of Christ. Instead, as Rowan Williams makes clear, "the recognizability of Jesus in the world is bound to the visible community *insofar as it is constituted by turning and returning to the foundational act of Christ*." From the beginning the Gospel has constituted a scandal and stumbling block, not only because of its claim to absoluteness and finality, but also because it proclaims Jesus' "foundational act" of solidarity with those who are most powerless and who seem most distant from God. Hence the Church's perpetual recourse to what Williams describes as its "principle of radical relativization of any claims it may make for itself and [thus its] radical Christ-centered judgment on its current life."[7]

[6] Cardinal Joseph Ratzinger, *Faith and the Future* (Chicago: Franciscan Herald Press, 1971), 117–18.

[7] Rowan Williams, *Christ the Heart of Creation* (New York: Bloomsbury Continuum, 2018), 76.

For the church to be made visible as "the form of Christ in the world" requires in fact that it occupy real times and spaces. Yet it will make no territorial claims, as if it had to contest with the world for a place within it. "The space of the church," declares Bonhoeffer, "is not there in order to fight with the world for a piece of its territory, but precisely to testify to the world that it is still the world, namely the world that is loved and reconciled by God." The former Archbishop of Canterbury thus summarizes Bonhoeffer's central ecclesial claim:

> So the Church is not simply a realm of reality, a subdivision, but a locus from which the world can be seen as a whole and responded to with a wholeness of service and compassion. The Church exists to say to the world that it need not be afraid of the Church, of a Church that seeks to displace or control it. . . . The irony in the Church's very being is that it is there to make a universal and comprehensive claim that has nothing to do with any aspiration to be a universal system of control. . . . Its particular system of interest, the corner it seeks to defend, is the interest of no specific group or party in exclusion or isolation.[8]

Hence Bonhoeffer's own conclusion: "There is no part of the world, no matter how lost, no matter how godless, that has not been accepted by God in Jesus Christ and reconciled to God."[9]

My central claim is that the life and work of Flannery O'Connor—her novels and stories, her letters and essays—are imbued with an understanding of the Church that deeply accords with that of Emeritus Pope Benedict XVI as well as Dietrich Bonhoeffer. Like them, she summons the Church to make visible its revolutionary witness at a time when it has become virtually occluded. Hence the following attempt to account for the Church's paradoxical invisibility.

8 Williams, *Christ the Heart of Creation*, 202.
9 Quoted by Williams, *Christ the Heart of Creation*, 201.

1

How the Church Became Invisible

A Christian Reading of American Literary Tradition[1]

It is surely a scandal that "a nation with the soul of a Church," as G. K. Chesterton famously described our country in *What I Saw in America* (1922), should have produced so few writers who are Christian in any substantive sense. Emerson, Thoreau, Dickinson, Melville, Poe, Hawthorne, Twain, James, Frost, Faulkner—nearly all of our eminent writers are heterodox at best or atheist at worst. T. S. Eliot doesn't count, since he became Christian after becoming a British citizen. Only such major-minor figures as Flannery O'Connor and Walker Percy can be regarded as distinctively Christian writers in America insofar as their artistic vision derives from the scandal of the Evangel. There is a seemingly obvious answer to this conundrum: Brilliant minds gifted with artistic imagination may have seen biblical faith as a snare and delusion and thus have refused to make its claims essential to their work. The task at hand is to state the counter-case that our major writers have had little substantive regard for Christianity because our churches have made it virtually impossible for them to do so.

As the only nation founded almost entirely on an Enlightenment basis, our country has nonetheless maintained an inveterate religiosity—exceeded perhaps only by that of India. Dana Gioia notes that our vaunted religious liberty did not issue in religiously arresting art:

> There was neither an established church nor an accepted orthodoxy. [Such] freedom was reflected in the individuality of the major poets. Ralph Waldo Emerson and Henry Wadsworth Longfellow followed

[1] Before my considerable revision of it, this chapter was originally published as "How the Church Became Invisible: A Christian Reading of American Literary Tradition" (with Stanley Hauerwas), in *Invisible Conversations: Religion in the Literature of America*, ed. Roger Lundin (Waco, Tex.: Baylor University Press, 2009), 159–86, 210–16.

> the Transcendentalist Zeitgeist into Unitarianism. Longfellow (like Tennyson) kept a residual reverence for Christ; but for Emerson, Jesus was no more divine than any other person. "Dare to love God without a mediator," he declared. Jesus still had reality for Emily Dickinson, but he was a comforter of her own making, in no way central to the pantheism and deism that animated her poetry. Other writers left Christianity entirely. Edgar Allan Poe professed an aesthetic idealism. Walt Whitman found divinity in every human being and nearly everything else in the world. The Protestant literary imagination had fragmented Christianity into the individual consciences of its believers and its doubters. In the process, Christ had mostly disappeared.[2]

We maintain, with Gioia, that our major literary artists have had but little imaginative regard for our churches. They have become literarily invisible because they have been so fully identified with the American project. After accounting for this strange invisibility, we will examine some of the ways in which Christians remain profoundly indebted to our national literary tradition despite its sub-Christian character.

The Gospel of Jesus Christ as the Gospel of the United States

Our first claim is that authentic Christian witness in American literature has been watery and thin because our churches, Catholic and Protestant alike, have often made the gospel of Jesus Christ seem all too much like the gospel of the United States. The trumpets of ecclesial America have been virtually indistinguishable from the nation's own buglers, leaving our major writers but little cause to regard Christ and the Kingdom as even the assumed background to their work. What a Jewish rabbi once confessed about his own faith, we believe to be true also for us Christians: "While America has been good for Jews," he said, "it has been bad for Judaism."[3] It is surely a good thing that Jews have not been subjected to American pogroms and holocausts, and that their talents and capacities have flourished here as virtually nowhere else in the world. And yet this new birth of freedom from persecution and for prosperity has often meant the ruin of Judaism as a radically communal and counter-cultural existence: the

[2] Dana Gioia, "Christianity and Poetry," *First Things*, August 2022, https://www.firstthings.com/article/2022/08/christianity-and-poetry.

[3] Manfred Vogel, in an unpublished lecture given at Wake Forest University in 1974.

life of the synagogue, the life devoted to things higher than, other than, and even opposed to cultural flourishing—in sum, the life of communal worship and service given to the one true God: Yahweh.

So it is with us Christians. Were it not for our brave ancestors who, at great risk, left the old world for the new, many of us would still be hammering rocks in Europe, living in perpetual peonage to our backs rather than our brains. Like our Jewish counterparts, however, we have too often equated American opportunity with the human good, yet with this notable difference: We have made American opportunity virtually coterminous with Christian freedom. Contra Chesterton, therefore, our churches have often had the soul of a nation. Rarely has the Christian herald sounded the good and therefore dangerous News that, though they indeed intersect and at times even coincide, the Church and the nation will always remain alternative regimes, occasionally overlapping but often scandalously conflicting. The city of God and the city of man can never be coterminous, as Augustine insisted a millennium and a half ago.

From Persecuted Minority to Established State Church

Such acculturation of the Gospel is not unique, of course, to Christianity in America. As Henri de Lubac observes, the early Church regarded the Eucharist as the mystical body of Christ while the gathered community was understood as the real body of Christ. The Real Presence lay not in the bread and wine alone so much as in the body of believers whose transubstantiation into a reconciled community was enabled by their partaking of the mystical meal. It transformed them into Christ's actual presence in the world, empowering them to live according to a drastically different Story than the world lives by. There they celebrated the true Narrative of the entire cosmos as it is sacramentally compressed into the singular Supper of suffering and death and resurrection. Gradually, however, these terms were reversed, so that the Eucharist alone was understood as the *real* Presence, while the Christian community became the far vaguer—and, alas, the often inert—thing called the *mystical* Body of Christ. The long-term result was that the Eucharist eventually became known as "the medicine of heaven," a quasi-pharmaceutical remedy against sin, often taken without serious regard for the communal reconciliation and transformation which it originally enabled.[4]

[4] De Lubac describes the original but soon-abandoned understanding of the Church: "If Christ is the sacrament of God, the Church is for us the sacrament of

Not long after the Emperor Constantine issued the Edict of Milan in 313, making Christianity a tolerated faith, the Church soon became the official cult of the Roman Empire. This reversal of the original order of things—granting immense new political power to Christians—also changed the locus of their confidence in God. Prior to Constantine's establishment of the Church as the state religion, as John Howard Yoder notes, Christians were convinced that God's action was to be discerned primarily in the Church, even as they also believed that God remains at work in the world. Yet in the face of Roman enmity, Christians had little confidence that God ordered the affairs of the Roman state; on the contrary, the Gospel alone sustained them as a community facing governmental torment.

After Constantine, however, Christians became ever more confident that God was active chiefly in the world, while only secondarily present in the Church. By the time of Theodosius II, only a century later, the reversal had been made complete: It became a civil offense *not* to be a Christian. And by the time of Charlemagne in the ninth century, this first Holy Roman Emperor had turned the Church into an organ of state power, using it to force the conversion of conquered peoples. From having suffered as a persecuted minority, to being tolerated as an accepted plurality, finally to reigning as the established majority religion, Christianity became the religious arm of the empire. The Gospel had thus been fundamentally transformed from a voluntary faith into a civic duty: To be Christian was the enforced obligation of every citizen of the Holy Roman Empire.

The Cultural Establishment of Christianity in America

This small discourse on the Constantinian-cum-Carolingian shift, as it is sometimes called, may seem to stand at a far remove from our concern

Christ; she represents him, in the full and ancient meaning of the term: she really makes him present. She not only carries on his work, but she is the very continuation, in a sense far more real than that in which it can be said that any human institution is the founder's continuation. The highly developed exterior organization that wins our admiration is but an expression, in accordance with the needs of this present life, of the interior unity of a living entity, so that the Catholic is not only subject to a power but is a member of a body as well, and his legal dependence on this power is to the end that he may have part in the life of that body. His submission in consequence is not an abdication, his orthodoxy is not mere conformity, but fidelity. It is not his duty to obey her orders or show deference to her counsels, but to share in a life, to enjoy a spiritual union" (*Catholicism: Christ and the Common Destiny of Man*, trans. Lancelot C. Sheppard and Sister Elizabeth Englund OCD [San Francisco: Ignatius Press, 1988], 76).

with American religion and literature. For, once the Puritan and Anglican attempts to create state churches ended in the eighteenth century, our national project was built on the explicit disavowal of any established religion, even Christianity. We believe, on the contrary, that the American churches have enjoyed a cultural establishment that, precisely for being subtle, may be far more pernicious than the old-style conflation of realms. Jefferson, for example, assumed that the nation would retain a Christian majority whose morality would undergird the enlightened political wisdom of such miracle-and-doctrine-denying deists as himself. Among the chief purposes of the state, according to Jefferson and his fellow Founders, was the need to save the nation from the contentious religious factions spawned by the Reformation. Like other *philosophes* of the Enlightenment, they sought to prevent a repetition of the sixteenth- and seventeenth-century "wars of religion" that required the state to settle disputes among bloody-minded believers. The only way to stop such internecine battles was to remove conflicting Christian doctrines and practices from the public realm, lest both Europe and the newly born American republic be bathed in religious gore yet again. Tolerance was the chief means for such religious peace, as it came to flower in the Treaty of Westphalia, in Locke's "Letter on Toleration," in Jefferson's "Notes on Virginia," and the like.

William Cavanaugh maintains that this standard account of the triumph of tolerance is wrongheaded. He demonstrates that the halting of the so-called "religious wars" was less a political necessity than a political convenience. According to Cavanaugh, Protestants killed Protestants and Catholics killed Catholics in the interest of the new power-configurations that developed after the demise of the medieval order. These "wars of religion," far from being internecine religious conflicts, marked the birth pangs of the sovereign nation-state. It became crucial, therefore, to redescribe both Protestantism and Catholicism. No longer were they understood as particularistic practices of Christianity, but rather as subspecies of a putatively more basic thing called "religion."

Religion came to be understood, in turn, as "beliefs," as essentially private convictions held quite apart from public loyalty to the state. Thus did the emerging nation-states thoroughly centralize political power in order, Cavanaugh argues, to provide "a monopoly on violence within a defined territory." Public discourse was deliberately secularized during the Enlightenment, he notes, in order to protect the state from the real threat posed by the churches: "Christianity produces divisions," writes

Cavanaugh, "within the state body precisely because it pretends to be a body which transcends state boundaries."[5]

Religious Freedom as Individual Self-Construction

The First Amendment to the U.S. Constitution obscures this paradoxical marginalizing of the churches. Because Christianity cannot be instituted by law, most Americans remain so accustomed to its cultural authority that legal disestablishment is unnecessary. Yet such Christian hegemony, for all its seemingly public character, remains at once peculiarly privatized and thus subtly coercive. Only when the main activities of the churches are safely confined to the religious sphere are they benignly to be "tolerated" by the state. Cavanaugh points to the ironic consequence of this new birth of tolerance—the hegemonic power of the state intolerantly to disbar all publicly ordered religions and all historically nourished traditions. The ideal of tolerance comes, in fact, to exclude the political and communal body of the Church, says Cavanaugh, "as a rival to the state body by redefining religion as a purely internal matter, an affair of the soul and not of the body."[6] "The creation of religion, and thus the privatization of the Church," Cavanaugh adds elsewhere, "is correlative to the rise of the state."[7]

It follows that the state alone, not the Church, can establish a true commonwealth, for religion now pertains chiefly to the newly constructed

5 William T. Cavanaugh, "The City: Beyond Secular Parodies," in *Radical Orthodoxy*, ed. John Milbank, Catherine Pickstock, and Graham Ward (New York: Routledge, 1999), 191, 189.

6 Cavanaugh, "The City," 192.

7 William T. Cavanaugh, *Theopolitical Imagination: Discovering the Liturgy as a Political Act in an Age of Global Consumerism* (New York: T&T Clark, 2002), 31.

Carolyn Marvin and David Ingle, in *Blood Sacrifice and the Nation* (Cambridge: Cambridge University Press, 1999), make Cavanaugh's point even more tellingly: "[I]n the religiously plural society of the United States, sectarian faith is optional for citizens, as everyone knows. Americans have rarely bled, sacrificed or died for Christianity or any other sectarian faith. Americans have often bled, sacrificed and died for their country. This fact is an important clue to the [nation's] religious power. Though denominations are permitted to exist in the United States, they are not permitted to kill, for their beliefs are not officially true. What is really true in any society is what is worth killing for and what citizens may be compelled to sacrifice their life for" (9).

When American Christians declare, as they often do, that "I believe that Jesus redeemed the world but that's only my personal opinion," all possibility of Christian resistance to state power has ended before it could even begin.

individual.[8] "The care of each man's soul belongs only to himself," wrote Locke.[9] "The legitimate powers of government," added Jefferson, "extend to such acts only as are injurious to others. But it does me no injury for my neighbor to say that there are twenty Gods, or no God. It neither picks my pocket nor breaks my leg."[10]

From such sentiments there emerges a triumphant individualism centered upon a new definition of freedom. In negative terms, liberty means doing no physical harm to others; in positive terms, it entails the construction of life as one so wills. No longer is freedom construed as obedience to a *telos* radically transcending ourselves and thus delivering us from bondage to mere self-interest. Rather is liberty to be found in a life lived according to one's own construal of reality. At its extreme, such individualism holds that one can make up one's identity entirely out of whole cloth, stripping away all bothersome particularities that locate one within concrete narrative traditions. One is free only as one rids oneself of those troublous commitments and obligations one has not chosen entirely for oneself. In sum, one is called to live as an individual immunized against all moral and social obligations except those that one has independently elected.[11]

[8] The invention of this word to mean "existing as a separate indivisible entity" is an entirely modern occurrence deriving from the seventeenth century. The word "person," by contrast, is ancient. For the Greeks, it meant mask or character, office or capacity; for Christians in the Middle Ages, it signified a human being. The Greeks found the notion of an individual self to be so subhuman that they called such a creature *idiōtēs*. Not to be a communal person is not to be a person at all, since we are human only insofar as we derive our existence from life together in the *polis*. The medievals, in turn, employed the word "idiot" in a similar fashion—namely, to signify a blockhead or a fool, a clown or a jester incapable of rational conduct.

For a critique of the entire idea of selfhood as something separate from the body political and physical, see Stanley Hauerwas, "The Sanctified Body: Why Perfection Does Not Require a 'Self,'" in *Sanctify Them in the Truth: Holiness Exemplified* (Nashville: Abingdon, 1998): 77–91.

[9] John Locke, "A Letter on Toleration" [1689], trans. William Popple, www.constitution.org/jl/tolerati.htm.

[10] Thomas Jefferson, "Notes on Virginia" (Boston: Lilly and Wait, 1832), accessed through the Library of Congress, https://www.loc.gov/item/03004902/.

[11] The single moral norm, it follows, is the injunction to respect the dignity of others by not denying them the freedom to exercise their own moral autonomy.

Michael J. Sandel notes that such procedural liberalism opposes "any view that regards us as obligated to fulfill ends that we have not chosen—ends given by nature or God, for example, or by our identities as members of families, peoples, cultures, or traditions. Encumbered identities such as these are at odds with the liberal conception of [persons] as free and independent selves, unbound by prior moral ties, capable of

The rise of the modern nation-state is premised, in fact, on the elevation of isolated and autonomous people who are largely defined by their accumulation of privately owned goods. As an essentially propertied creature, modern individuals have relation to other individuals primarily by means of self-protecting contracts. These contracts have only a temporal duration, in turn, even as they are also contingent on the agreement of the contracting parties. Contracts can also be dissolved by limiting clauses as well as by mutual consent. No longer is there an unbreakable bond uniting community members, much less the entire body politic, in devotion to common ends. The very basis of such a politics has also disappeared—namely, the indissoluble covenant between God and his people, as this bond is sealed through the sacraments. "It is not surprising," Cavanaugh writes, "that . . . Descartes placed 'among the [antique] excesses all of the promises by which one curtails something of one's freedom,' that Milton wrote a treatise on divorce, or that Kant condemned the covenants that bind one's descendants."[12]

The Modern Triumph of Pietistic Individualism

Let our intent be clear: We are not denying that acculturated Christianity is still a form of Christianity. Without it, we confess, many of us would not be Christians at all. Even so, we insist that it is a terribly truncated form of the Faith and that our major American writers have had good cause for not employing it as the animating center or even the assumed background of their work. Moralistic liberalism and individualistic pietism are the mirror evils, we also contend, that have made the Church understood as the distinctive Body of Christ virtually invisible in America.

The nineteenth- and twentieth-century pietism that caused our major American writers to turn away in scorn if not wrath is but a distant kinsman of its seventeenth- and eighteenth-century predecessor. In both Europe and the United States, the original pietists were both anti-hegemonic and politically engaged Christians, offering a powerful corrective to a nominal and accommodationist kind of Christianity that had been reduced to

---

choosing our ends for ourselves. This is the conception that finds expression in the ideal of the state as a neutral framework. . . . a framework of rights that refuses to choose among competing values and ends. For the liberal self, what matters above all, what is most essential to our personhood, is not the ends we choose but our capacity to choose them" (*Democracy's Discontent: America in Search of a Public Philosophy* [Cambridge, Mass.: Belknap Press, 1996], 12).

12 Cavanaugh, "The City," 190.

mere formal reception of the sacraments, mere verbal assent to creeds, mere outward adherence to liturgical worship. These early pietists sought to recover the original vitality of the Reformers—in their deeply personal and experiential faith, in their prophetic preaching for the sake of conversion and sanctification, in their confidence that the indwelling Spirit could commend the truth of Scripture to the hearts and lives of the unlearned, in their vigorous opposition to slavery, in their courageous promotion of prison reform, in their evangelistic and missionary zeal, in their creation of Sunday schools and Bible societies and colleges, in their advocacy of the freedom of conscience, in their emphasis on the centrality of the laity for the life of the Church, etc. Yet the pietism that began as a minority countermovement in the seventeenth and eighteenth centuries triumphed in the nineteenth and twentieth centuries as our quasi-official form of national Christianity.[13]

Timothy Smith, Joel Carpenter, Nathan Hatch, and others have hailed religious voluntarism as the genius of American Christianity. That citizens are legally free rather than required to join any or no particular church is surely a great good. Not only has it liberated our churches to carry out the Great Commission by evangelizing non-Christians; it has also enabled the converted to enact serious social reforms. Yet this voluntarism has often been purchased at an enormous and usually unrecognized price. It places such drastic emphasis on individual conversion and private piety that the churches often become afterthoughts, the places where one seeks merely to confirm what really counts: one's private and spiritual relation to God.

William Portier points out that such pietist evangelicalism also assumes a Lockean view of the Church as a voluntary association of individuals as well as a metaphysics that gives ontological priority to human will over the created order. The unintended consequence of such religious pluralism is that the churches which embrace it become both individualistic and anti-institutional:

> Pluralism encourages voluntary churches but puts them in the incongruous position of having to develop theories to explain how they can be "public." The correlative of public is of course private. This means that the seemingly unprecedented field for

[13] We owe this summary of pietism to Barry Harvey's *Politics of the Theological: Beyond the Piety and Power of a World Come of Age* (New York: Peter Lang, 1995), 39–45. Perhaps the definitive history of this movement is still F. Ernest Stoeffler's *The Rise of Evangelical Pietism* (Leiden: Brill, 1965).

> evangelization [that] pluralism offers is always simultaneously undermined by its corresponding notion that voluntary churches occupy "private" space.[14]

Even as modern political conditions encourage evangelical forms, they also tend to deform Christianity insofar as it is meant to be made ecclesial and incarnate within particular cultures. Modern notions of tolerance tend to domesticate both the Christianity that is being preached and the form of life that it entails by treating them simply as one among many private "religions." Soon religious pluralism is transformed from a providential fact into a theoretical good, a natural state of things best left undisturbed. If pluralism is a natural state, missionaries are imperialists. Evangelists who take Matthew 28:19 seriously are accused of imposing their private beliefs on others. The cry "Woe is me if I do not preach the gospel" (1 Cor 9:16 NKJV) turns Paul into an oppressor.

The Danger of Moralistic Innocence

Concerning our inveterate moralism, R. W. B. Lewis argued a generation ago, in *The American Adam*, that Melville and James joined Hawthorne's protest against the dangerous complacency endemic to moralistic American innocence. It leads to a reformist understanding of human nature as being so malleable that it can be reshaped into a veritable mechanism of righteousness.[15] So did Lionel Trilling, himself a venerable liberal, lament already in the late 1940s that America has had no other cultural tradition than liberalism. "In the United States at this time liberalism is not only the dominant but even the sole intellectual tradition. For it is a plain fact that nowadays there are no conservative or reactionary ideas in general circulation." Trilling the liberal offered his magisterial judgment not boastfully but regretfully. He complained that, in its prosaic desire to enlarge human freedom through the rational organization of life, liberalism neglects the

[14] William Portier, "Here Come the Evangelical Catholics," *Communio* 31 (Spring 2004): 42–43. Portier offers a caveat that we also affirm: "The point of such critique [of modern pluralism] is not to advocate doing away with legal tolerance but to show its limits and to exhort Christians to transcend it." Barry Harvey maintains that three twentieth-century Baptists—Walter Rauschenbusch, Martin Luther King Jr., and Clarence Jordan—were sustained by such a radically prophetic and counter-hegemonic pietism.

[15] R. W. B. Lewis, *The American Adam* (Chicago: University of Chicago Press, 1959).

poetic "imagination of variousness and possibility, which implies the awareness of complexity and difficulty." Liberals often forget, Trilling warned, that "the world is a complex and unexpected and terrible place."[16] Like Lewis, Trilling feared that our moralistic optimism about human nature and destiny had robbed many Americans, including many American writers, of any radical capacity for self-criticism.

So did Robert Penn Warren bemoan this same Yankee confidence in the "Treasury of Virtue," as he labeled it, this fund of moral righteousness that Northerners credited to themselves for having put a stop to slavery. The Civil War gave the victors such a shining sense of millennial destiny for the American republic that, in revulsion against such Yankee triumphalism, post-Appomattox writers of the South retreated into what Louis Simpson calls "a politics of apology or justification . . . [of] a defeated national polity. . . . an aborted national will."[17] He cites such Lost Cause poets as William Gilmore Simms and Thomas Nelson Page as its chief apologists.

Against such reactionism, Simpson argues that, from Thoreau forward, there was a steady defection of "the most literary minds from society, as the man of letters assumed the role of prophet-priest-artist. At once a man of solitude and a member of a community . . . of literary alienation, he is a figure often absurd yet heroic."[18] Thenceforth our major American writers would locate "the sense of transcendent literary autonomy within [themselves]."[19] The result of this cataclysmic cultural shift is that inner self-transcendence becomes what Simpson describes as "the major literary resource of modern times."[20] Yet the Southern Agrarians prided themselves on refusing this Great Literary Secession. They envisioned the Old South as a traditionalist society, a homogeneous community that preserved, as Donald Davidson declared, the "eighteenth century European America that is elsewhere forgotten."[21]

It was a huge deceit, of course, a whole-cloth confection, as Simpson demonstrates. Southern slavery had little in common with traditionalist societies. Slavery was a supremely modern and capitalist enterprise,

16 Lionel Trilling, *The Liberal Imagination: Essays on Literature and Society* (New York: Viking Press, 1950), preface.

17 Louis P. Simpson, *The Man of Letters in New England and the South* (Baton Rouge: Louisiana State University Press), 242.

18 Simpson, *Man of Letters*, 235.

19 Simpson, *Man of Letters*, 234.

20 Simpson, *Man of Letters*, 235.

21 Quoted in Simpson, *Man of Letters*, 251.

especially with the invention of the cotton gin. The Southern economy fully participated in what Simpson calls "the leading force of American history—an evolving technological materialism."[22] He shows that the Southern Agrarians did not avoid the Great Literary Secession. Exactly to the contrary, they were its very epigoni. Borrowing from Henry James Sr., he concludes that these *soi-disant* Agrarians deceived themselves into believing "that their primary literary inheritance was not agonizingly self-conscious and ideological but traditional, that the Old South constituted a traditionalist order."[23]

Emily Dickinson as Faithful Non-Convert Poet

Emily Dickinson was the legatee of both moralism and pietism, well before the Civil War and the frontier revivals had established their admixture as the nation's unofficial religion. It left her unable to embrace Christian faith—not, we believe, because she had encountered its authentic expression and found it wanting, but rather because they prompted her to take refuge in religious individualism: She became a recluse to avoid being conscripted for an allegedly Christian cause that she knew to be dubious at best, spurious at worst.

During her single year of college life at the Mount Holyoke Female Seminary, the seventeen-year-old Dickinson was tutored by the school's founder, the redoubtable Mary Lyon. Like other Whig evangelicals of her day, Lyon envisioned Christianity as forming a powerful tandem with science and education for bringing about a moral revolution of the entire planet. The Kingdom of heaven was soon to come on earth—if not in the nineteenth then surely in the twentieth century, which would so certainly become the *Christian Century* that a still-existing journal was thus named. In an 1842 address setting forth this confident evangelicalism, Lyon envisioned a time rapidly approaching when all people would "act according to the principles of reason and religion," when "all that now goes into the war channel, will then be consecrated to the service of knowledge and benevolence."[24]

The key to such moral transformation lay in the punctiliar act of becoming a Christian via a sudden and emotional conversion experience.

22 Simpson, *Man of Letters*, 238.

23 Simpson, *Man of Letters*, 248.

24 Roger Lundin, *Emily Dickinson and the Art of Belief* (Grand Rapids: Eerdmans, 1998), 37.

Such a dramatic rebirth was public proof that one had personally appropriated the gift of divine grace. A miraculous conversion was the spiritual equivalent of the physical violations of nature that were said to be miraculous evidences of God's existence. "In working toward the conversion of her students at Mount Holyoke," Roger Lundin writes, "Lyon divided them each year into three groups." The "Christians" were those who could testify to the certainty of their salvation experience. The "Hopers" believed themselves to be on the verge of conversion. The "No-Hopers," by contrast, could not attest to any drastic emotional reversal that demonstrated their faith in Christ.[25]

Emily Dickinson was numbered on the short list of souls called No-Hopers. They were the special targets of fervent evangelical attention at Mount Holyoke and Amherst alike. Dickinson remained one of the few holdouts. "How lonely this world is growing," she wrote in the spring of 1850. "Christ is calling everyone here [. . .], and I am standing alone in rebellion, and growing very careless."[26] To her friend Abiah Root, Dickinson confessed that "I have perfect confidence in God & his promises and yet I know not why, I feel that the world holds a predominant place in my affections. I do not feel that I could give up all for Christ, were I called to die."[27]

That Dickinson refused such a public profession of faith does not mean, as Lundin makes clear, that she was an atheist scoffer. On the contrary, Dickinson admitted "that I shall never be happy without I love Christ."[28] Yet if the love of Christ were signified by an overwhelmingly subjective conversion, Dickinson did not want it. And if the world's wonders were to be disvalued, Dickinson would not do so. Yet the Jesus of the gospels who remained so dear to Dickinson demanded no such emotional upheavals, no such denials of the good creation. The outward claims of Christian faith were not therefore her chief worry. What vexed Dickinson were her own uncontrollable and often delusory emotions. To her friend Root, she thus explained her refusal to attend the Amherst revival meetings of 1850: "I felt that I was so easily excited that I might again be deceived and I dared not trust myself."[29]

25 Lundin, *Emily Dickinson and the Art of Belief*, 40–41.

26 Lundin, *Emily Dickinson and the Art of Belief*, 49.

27 Quoted in D. Bruce Lockerbie, *Dismissing God: Modern Writers' Struggle Against Religion* (Grand Rapids: Eerdmans, 1999), 41.

28 Lundin, *Emily Dickinson and the Art of Belief*, 49.

29 Lundin, *Emily Dickinson and the Art of Belief*, 49.

An established Christianity seeking to force Emily Dickinson's conversion could not possibly win her permanent esteem. Nor could an acculturated Christianity countenance the intellectual difficulties and theological qualms that prompted Dickinson's refusal to be converted. It contained little room for the recalcitrant doubt which, from Job forward, has signaled a radical desire for faith. The same Protestant individualism that failed to convert Dickinson prompted her to conceive of her poetic integrity as something she would have to surrender if she became a professed Christian. Why should she have thought otherwise? Given this heretical dichotomy, Dickinson was surely right to refuse such an allegedly heroic act of autonomous will, such a gnostic denial of the good creation, such a subjective enthusiasm requiring ever-new infusions of emotion. Dickinson is to be commended rather than condemned for daring not trust herself to inward upheavals. In rejecting the deity of nineteenth-century Protestant piety, she did not minimize her soul's experience so much as she expanded it. Indeed, Dickinson became one of our most important poets of the spiritual life, not another of the dreary and virtually unreadable pietists of her time.

"This World Is Not Conclusion"

Number 501 is a poem at once sprightly and memorable because it is at once troubling and edifying. Here Dickinson sets forth an arrestingly perceptive understanding of the relation between faith and doubt:

> This World is not Conclusion.
> A Species stands beyond—
> Invisible, as Music—
> But positive, as Sound—
> It beckons, and it baffles—
> Philosophy, don't know—
> And through a Riddle, at the last—
> Sagacity, must go—
> To guess it, puzzles scholars—
> To gain it, Men have borne
> Contempt of Generations
> And Crucifixion, shown—
> Faith slips—and laughs, and rallies—
> Blushes, if any see—
> Plucks at a twig of Evidence—
> And asks a Vane, the way—

Much Gesture, from the Pulpit—
Strong Hallelujahs roll—
Narcotics cannot still the Tooth
That nibbles at the soul—

The pseudo-deity of triumphalist pietism who can be known within worldly categories offers his disciples the blessings of finite faith, the comforts of mundane assurance. The true God, by contrast, dwells within the world while standing beyond it, the Reality unseen as music yet real as sound. This unknown God who alone can make himself known both attracts and repels, both frightens and captivates. When ensconced in airy abstractions, such false faith can comprehend everything under the sun but the most important thing: the Mystery who is the real God.

Eluding all such confining categories, the God Who Is prompts an honestly agnostic "don't know." The world's wisdom, even at best, is a set of riddles and conundrums. Airy academics, with their dry distinctions, can only speculate about this Species who belongs to no genus. Those who actually gain Reality must lose their lives in grappling with the unobvious God, either dying to themselves in daily martyrdom or else suffering the contempt of cultured and uncultured despisers of doubt-filled faith.

Such faith always entails radical risk. It is never something as clear and certain as a proposition. It is an affair of slipping and advancing, of losing and rallying, of weeping and rejoicing. So shy of self-confidence is true faith that it blushes when asked to expound its own piety. John Calvin himself would say no more than that he had come to saving faith *subita conversione*, in a sudden reversal of his life's path. Knowing that God's own self-identification in Israel and Christ is the only basis for their existence, Christians put no more weight on subjective experience than a twig might bear, and as sinners constituting the tattered Bride of Christ, they receive but dubious direction from the wind-blown cock atop Puritan churches. The real Gospel is meant to announce the Resurrection, of course, but this steepled vane blows with every wind of doctrine, even as its cock may crow with suspicious eroticism. Despite the flailing of perfervid preachers and the praise-songs of easy believers, true Faith is never free from the toothache of doubt.

The feel-good pharmacists of the No-God[30] offer vain narcotics to ease the pain sent by the true God. The real Lord will not anesthetize shallow

[30] Cf. Karl Barth's denunciation of what he calls the No-God of a merely civil faith. Barth regards this pseudo-divinity as the most pernicious of all human inventions because it stanches any radical transformation of either persons or

souls with worldly finalities, even of the most "spiritual" sort. Instead, he implants the molar of doubt no less than the tusk of truth, and they gnaw at the soul like a mouse at cheese. This God is not Blake's Old Nobodaddy, not Hemingway's Our Nada Who Art in Nada, not the Big Guy in the Sky whose death we ought, instead, to celebrate. This, instead, is the God whose Son was himself wracked by doubt in Gethsemane, in fear and trembling that his Kingdom would come only as he mounted the bloody Tree from which he would rule the world by reconciliation rather than coercion.

Conclusion

It will be evident that we have been following St. Augustine's injunction that Christians should "take the spoils of the Egyptians"—making Christian use of the excellent accomplishments found in the non-Christian world (*On Christian Doctrine*, book 2, chapter 40, section 60). Whatever enables Christians to live more faithfully as a storied community over against all unstoried autonomy—and thus against the domination and coercion that such storyless autonomy produces—this we must claim unabashedly as our own. Christian interpreters of American literature should follow the example of John Howard Yoder, we believe, in his insistence that "the humanity of Jesus was a cultural reality."

> Far from transcending history, he was a first-century Jewish rabbi who made disciples precisely within his and their own culture. Just as Jesus retained almost all of his own Judaism, rejecting only those Jews who sought a Messiah who would replace Roman force with Jewish force, so must Jesus' contemporary followers exercise a sim-

---

communities. Such a god, says Barth, confirms "the course of the world and of men as it is." Belief in this comforting and consoling deity is ever so difficult to surrender:

> We suppose that we know what we are saying when we say "God." We assign to Him the highest place in our world: and in so doing we place Him on fundamentally one line with ourselves and with things. We assume that He needs something: and so we assume that we are able to arrange our relation to Him as we arrange other relationships. We press ourselves into proximity with Him: and so, all unthinking, we make Him nigh unto ourselves. We allow ourselves an ordinary communication with Him, we permit ourselves to reckon with Him as though this were not extraordinary behaviour on our part. We dare to deck ourselves out as His companions, patrons, advisers, and commissioners. We confound time with eternity. (*The Epistle to the Romans*, 6th ed., trans. Edwyn C. Hoskyns [New York: Oxford University Press, 1968], 40, 44)

> ilar discernment concerning American literature, repenting of our hegemonic misdeeds, embracing authors and texts that are congruent with the faith, declining to affirm those that are not.[31]

Yet where if at all in our national literature do we encounter writers whose work gives imaginative life, even if indirectly, to the Gospel and thus to the Church as the one transformative community? Where are there ecclesial communities that, by overcoming the triumphalist lure, are able to reconcile enemies and thus to empower their mutual resistance against the coercions of state and culture alike, whether social or psychological, whether economic or military? Where, even if partially and inadequately, are there fictional echoes and reflections of this baptismal and eucharistic people in whom the presence and power of their Messiah-Redeemer is alive and at work in their midst? Where is the triune God fashioning an alternative history for all people—indeed, for his whole creation? Where may writers be found who do not turn inward to locate "the sense of transcendent literary autonomy within themselves" but who turn outward to the Church and the world to find true Transcendence?

This book is devoted to the life and work of Flannery O'Connor as America's strongest literary witness to radical Christian faith. Yet first we must turn to Willa Cather's *Death Comes for the Archbishop* and *The Professor's House* as exceptions proving the rule that the Church remains all but invisible in American literature.

[31] We acknowledge that Yoder's theology is shadowed by his reprehensible moral life as it was revealed after his death. We make no defense of it whatsoever. We note only that, if his abominations were made the basis for rejecting the work of other premier writers and thinkers, little of their wisdom would be left.

Christians are summoned, says Yoder, to "represent within society, through and in spite of withdrawal from certain of its activities, as well as through and in spite of involvement with others, a real judgment upon the rebelliousness of culture and a real possibility of reconciliation for all" (quoted in Fritz Oehlschlaeger, *Love and Good Reasons: Postliberal Approaches to Christian Ethics and Literature* [Durham, N.C.: Duke University Press, 2003], 276, n. 40).

Oehlschlaeger makes an especially convincing case for the Christian appropriation of Henry James' fiction as an aid to moral discernment. So subtle and wise is James' depiction of motive and character that he helps Christians remain faithful to their own narrative and communal understanding of the ways in which the virtues are formed. In this regard at least, Henry Jr. was far more orthodox than his gnostically inclined father: "For James Sr., Creation is no longer second-order language [i.e., doctrinal speech] pointing to our contingency, to our existence's being a gift, to our participation in a story authored by God. Rather, it has become a philosophical abstraction, completely removed from temporal understanding or display" (39).

2

The Surprising Witness of Willa Cather in *Death Comes for the Archbishop* and *The Professor's House*

If it is ironic that, as a literary loner on the American scene, Flannery O'Connor has made the Church both visible and audible in her work, it is even more ironic that the most authentic portrayal of the Church in American literature is located not in the center but on the boundary of the nation's cultural life, and not in a Protestant but a Catholic community.[1] In Willa Cather's *Death Comes for the Archbishop*, the Church is brought forth from the shadows of what I have called its surprising invisibility. Cather happily confessed that the writing of this narrative gave her more joy than all her other works, and that abandoning Fathers Latour and Vaillant at the end was like a painful parting with old friends. Having made several visits to New Mexico, there to absorb all she could learn about Archbishop Lamy and his cathedral, visiting dozens of little adobe churches in surrounding towns, she penned her narrative in only a few months. It had a painless birth "because the book had been lived many times before it was written, and the happy mood in which I began it never paled."[2]

Willa Cather's Aestheticism

Before turning to this seminal work, it is important to note that it marks a notable departure from Cather's novels. What we find there is a high humanism imbued with an unabashed devotion to art as its own end—in short, to an unapologetic aestheticism. Like Lionel Trilling, Cather lamented the spiritual and aesthetic thinness of her progressivist era, the

1 I have considerably revised and expanded this essay.

2 Willa Cather, *Willa Cather on Writing* (New York: Knopf, 1949), 10.

liberalism that expended itself almost entirely on worthy social causes, largely to the neglect of religious complexity and artistic depth. The churches having offered her but little alternative, Cather drew her artistic inspiration largely from an idealism that centered upon individual sympathy and noble striving. "The world is little, people are little, human life is little," declares Wunsch in *The Song of the Lark*. "There is only one big thing," he adds, "—desire. And before it, when it is big, all is little."[3]

"Desire," declares Godfrey the epicurean protagonist of *The Professor's House*, "is creation, is the magical element in that process. If there were an instrument by which to measure desire, one could foretell achievement." He adds that "Art and religion (they are the same thing in the end, of course) have given man the only happiness he has ever had."[4] Those imbued with desire make new worlds for themselves, however illusory, while those who lack it sink into the deadness of various conformities. Hence Cather's artistic attention to pioneers of both the land and the spirit, those who discover the infinite resources available to them in both nature and art. "The pioneer needs imagination," the narrator announces in *O Pioneers!*, "in order to enjoy the idea of things more than things themselves."[5] Against the grain of her age, therefore, Cather was drawn to the definition of human happiness that she first articulated in *My Ántonia*, a motto that is also inscribed on her gravestone in New Hampshire: Happiness is "to become a part of something entire, whether it is sun and air, goodness and knowledge. . . . to be dissolved into something complete and great."

"Religion," Myra Henshaw declares to Father Fay in *My Mortal Enemy*, "is different from everything else; because in religion seeking is finding. . . . She seemed to say [the narrator explains] that in other searchings it might be the object of the quest that brought satisfaction, or it might be something incidental that one got on the way; but in religion, desire [is] fulfillment, it [is] the seeking itself which [is] rewarded."[6] "Art is not thought or emotion, but expression, expression, always expression. To keep an idea

[3] Willa Cather, *The Song of the Lark*, The Willa Cather Scholarly Edition (Lincoln: University of Nebraska Press, 2012), chap. 9, unpaginated.

[4] Willa Cather, *The Professor's House* (New York: Vintage Classics, 1990 [1925]), 55.

[5] Willa Cather, *O Pioneers!* The Willa Cather Scholarly Edition (Lincoln: University of Nebraska Press, 2012), chap. 5, unpaginated.

[6] Willa Cather, *My Mortal Enemy*, The Willa Cather Scholarly Edition (Lincoln: University of Nebraska Press, 2012), chap. 9, unpaginated.

living, intact, tinged with all its original feeling, its original mood, preserving it in all the ecstasy which attended its birth, to keep it so all the way from the brain to the hand and to transfer it on paper a living thing with color, odor, sound, life all in it, that is what art means, that is the greatest of all gifts of the gods. And that is the voyage perilous."[7] Cather's essay on Carlyle clinches the case that she worshiped at the altar of art: "Art of every kind is an exacting master, more so even than Jehovah. He says only, 'Thou shalt have no other Gods before me.' Art, science and letters cry, 'Thou shalt have no other Gods at all.' They accept only human sacrifices."[8]

Yet on two notable occasions, Willa Cather deviated from her ingrained aestheticism, most obviously in *Death Comes for the Archbishop* but also, albeit briefly and subtly, in *The Professor's House*. On both occasions she employed the powers of her sympathetic imagination in order that her characters might make a distinctively Christian witness.

Death Comes for the Archbishop

Willa Cather insisted on calling *Death Comes for the Archbishop* a narrative rather than a novel. It was not because a narrative freed Cather to do as she pleased, but because a novel depends on sheer invention rather than historical evidence. A novel is "a work of imagination in which the writer [tests] present experiences and emotions of a group of people by the light of his own."[9] Something revolutionary was required, by contrast, something radically experimental in creating *Death Comes for the Archbishop*. As if to confess that, in depicting the faithful lives of an archbishop and his vicar in the New World she was entering territory not entirely reducible to art, she abandoned almost all conventional fictional devices—plot, suspense, foreshadowing, and the like. Hence her decision not to proceed chronologically but episodically, not to withhold the story's final outcome but to announce it in the title itself.

This is not to say that the work lacks artistic structure.[10] On the contrary, the prologue in Rome is mirrored with a final remembrance of the France that the archbishop and his vicar had left behind forty years earlier. There

7 Willa Cather, "The Kingdom of Art," *Nebraska State Journal* (1 March 1896), 167–68, 354–56, 415–17.

8 Willa Cather, *The Hesperian* 22 (1891): 3–4.

9 Cather, *Cather on Writing*, 12–13.

10 In the final chapters, Cather might have been more novelistic and less narratistic. She puts off the Archbishop's death by indulging in endless invented diversions and divagations that add little if anything to the matter at hand.

is also a miracle recounted near the beginning and again near the end. The saintliness of Latour and Vaillant is also set in sharp relief by the corruption of the various other bishops and priests. Cather also creates a clear opposition between the Indians and the Americans, much to the detriment of the newcomers. Latour and Vaillant also form a fine complementary pair—Latour the keen-minded man, handsome and artistic; Vaillant the practical man, homely and indifferent to beauty. Yet such parallels and balances are not artificial devices so much as signs that the Christian life requires something far less dramatic, something steadier and more ordinary—namely, the fortitude marked by daily religious discipline within the Church. Knowing well that evil seems intrinsically more interesting than good, and that goodness is difficult to make artistically convincing, Cather dared nonetheless to hold her readers' interest via two saintly priests.

Insofar as her narrative had literary origins, it was to be found in the hagiographies recorded in *The Golden Legend.*[11] Its stories lack dramatic climaxes and descents. They impressed Cather, not because the fantastic miracles that the saints allegedly performed are portrayed startlingly, but because the martyrdoms that they actually suffered are narrated casually, as if they were ordinary occurrences. The death of the saints, Cather learned, are but the culmination and summation of their lives.

Archbishop Jean-Marie Latour and His Vicar General

Cather modeled Archbishop Jean-Marie Latour and his vicar Father Joseph Vaillant on both the celebrated "Apostle of Santa Fé," Jean-Baptiste Lamy, as well as his vicar-general Joseph Machebeuf. Her knowledge of the historical Lamy is not clear, but it is clear that her fictional portrait of him is highly idealized. His personal disposition was far from that of the saintly Latour. In his massive biography of Lamy, the Catholic novelist Paul Horgan discloses his many warts and wens:

> Cather invented Lamy's relationship to Indian culture, along with the vignettes and Indian friendships to sustain it. In fact, Lamy seems to have thought of Indians as violent, predatory threats, on the one hand, and as the objects of failed mission-school efforts

[11] Compiled circa 1260 by Jacobus de Voragine, a scholarly friar and later archbishop of Genoa, *The Golden Legend* was perhaps the most widely read book, after the Bible, during the late Middle Ages. Voragine sought to captivate, encourage, and edify the faithful while preserving a vast store of data pertaining to the legends and traditions of the church.

> on the other. Lamy's opposition to the reservation policy is also fiction, not history. So, too, apparently, his criticism of slavery. The one reference to slavery in the history is a favorable one made by Lamy's fellow-priest and lifelong companion, Joseph Machebeuf. The historical Lamy promoted the railroad and other instruments of Yankee progress; newcomers blamed him for changing the traditional Southwest.[12]

Yet in one brief scene Cather does have Latour echo Lamy's scorn for Indians as "violent, predatory threats." There the archbishop recounts the legend of Fray Baltazar concerning the Ácoma Indians. Dwelling atop their nearly impregnable mesa, they have become spiritually obdurate—hardened not only against Christian culture but, as the Archbishop observes, against transformation of any kind at all: "Through all the centuries that his own [European] part of the world had been changing like the sky at daybreak, this people had been fixed, increasing neither in numbers nor desires, rock-turtles on their rock. Something reptilian he felt here, something that had endured by immobility, a kind of life out of reach, like the crustaceans in their armour."[13]

Great Desert Spaces, Magnificent Open Skies, Majestic Mesas

There is nothing immobile or crustacean about Cather's narrative. She *inhabits* both the landscape and the persons of her narrative. She enters into them; she dwells inside rather than outside them. Her poetic powers give metaphysical heft to the carnelian hills and ochre mountains of New Mexico. Their barren beauty becomes transcendently real. Archbishop Latour's meditations on New Mexico's great desert spaces and magnificent open skies and stark rock formations are especially affecting. The mesas, he noted, seem like the Church itself in its antiquity and incompleteness; they are akin to vast Gothic cathedrals waiting to be finished, yet having their own integrity of sky and stone,

> as if, with all the materials for world-making assembled, the Creator had desisted, gone away and left everything on the point of being brought together, on the eve of being arranged into mountain, plain, plateau. The country was still waiting to be made into a landscape....

12 Michael Rogan, "Lamy of Santa Fé," *New York Times*, October 5, 1975.

13 Willa Cather, *Death Comes for the Archbishop* (New York: Vintage, 1997 [1927]), 103. Further citations will be contained within parentheses.

> The great tables of granite set down in an empty plain were inconceivable without their attendant clouds, which were part of them, as the smoke is part of the censer, or the foam of the wave. (94–95)

In comparison to such God-made natural glories, the archbishop observes that civilizations are built on the conquest of nature via cities whose massive structures attest to human mastery of the world. Over against them Latour marks the counter-attitudes and practices of the Indians:

> When they left the rock or tree or sand dune that sheltered them for the night, the Navajo was careful to obliterate every trace of their temporary occupation. He buried the embers of the fire and the remnants of food, unpiled any stones he had piled together, filled up the holes he had scooped in the sand. . . . Father Latour judged that, just as it was the white man's way to assert himself in any landscape, to change it, make it over a little (at least to leave some mark of memorial of his sojourn), it was the Indian's way to pass through a country without disturbing anything; to pass and leave no trace, like fish through water, or birds through air.
>
> This was not so much from indolence, the Bishop thought, as from an inherited caution and respect. It was as if the great country were asleep, and they wished to carry on their lives without awakening it; or as if the spirits of earth and air and water were things not to antagonize and arouse. . . . The land and all that it bore they treated with consideration; not attempting to improve it, they never desecrated it. (233–34)

Fear and Terror in an Underground River

Yet there is a price to be paid for having no critical distance from nature. It opens the Indians to worship its dark underside. In one of the narrative's most disturbing episodes, the Archbishop encounters something frighteningly primordial in the Indian worship of a giant snake-like river. Father Latour and his Navajo guide Jacinto have found refuge from a fierce snowstorm in a cave that had once been the secret site of Indian worship. Jacinto allows the Archbishop to enter only after swearing him to secrecy. Though the towering cavern reminds Latour of a Gothic chapel, he feels an instant repugnance for the place, perhaps because blood sacrifice had apparently been performed there. He is troubled not only by the fusty odor permeating the frigid air, but also by the cave's "extraordinary vibration," a noise humming "like a hive of bees, like a heavy roll of distant drums" (129). The droning sound causes Latour's head to swirl in dizzying confusion. Jacinto then invites the bishop to put his ear to a secret fissure in a wall of the cave, so that he too may hear the deep underground roar of this primordial river:

> The water was far, far below, perhaps as deep as the foot of the mountain, a flood moving in utter blackness under ribs of antediluvian rock. It was not a rushing noise, but the sound of a great flood moving with majesty and power.
>
> "It is terrible," he said at last, as he rose.
>
> "Sí, padre." Jacinto began spitting on the clay he had gouged out of the seam, and plastered it up again. (130)

Rebecca West noted that a writer such as D. H. Lawrence would have attempted to penetrate the crack in the wall and to pursue both the snake and the river, offering the reader a direct encounter with chthonic terror and might.[14] Instead, Cather narrates the portentous scene wholly from Latour's perspective. In so doing, she enables the reader to share his discernment that such immemorial Force antedates not only Christianity but civilization itself—and that it lies completely beyond their control. Though the cave had perhaps saved his life, Father Latour always remembers it "with horror" (133). No wonder that, during his single night there, the Archbishop makes sure to "read his breviary long by the light of the fire" (131). Nor does he later contest the candid judgment of an American trader: "No white man knows anything about Indian religion, Padre" (134). Only indigenous peoples have commerce with such uncontrollable Power.

The Blessed Amenities of Civilization

In her critique of the Western and Cartesian urge to subdue nature for human use, Willa Cather might seem to be a back-to-earth advocate. Yet she makes the Archbishop thoroughly Christian in his conviction that man is not meant to live, *per impossible*, in naive identity with nature:

14 Rebecca West, "The Classic Artist," in *Willa Cather and Her Critics*, ed. James Schroeter (Ithaca, N.Y.: Cornell University Press, 1967), 68. Hence West's caustic rhetorical question: "Does not such transcendental [Lawrentian] courage, does not such ambition to extend consciousness beyond its present limits and elevate man above himself, entitle his art to be ranked as more important than that of Miss Cather?"

> Father Latour's recreation was his garden. He grew such fruit as was hardly to be found even in the old orchards of California; cherries and apricots, apples and quinces, and the peerless pears of France—even the most delicate varieties. He urged the new priests to plant fruit trees wherever they went, and to encourage the Mexicans to add fruit to their starchy diet. Wherever there was a French priest, there should be a garden of fruit trees and vegetables and flowers. He often quoted to his students that passage from their fellow Auvergnat, Pascal: that Man was lost and saved in a garden. (265)

Finely prepared meals, according to the cultivated Archbishop, form the fundament of high cultures. After enjoying an especially flavorful dinner prepared by Vaillant, Latour observes that "soup like this is not the work of one man. It is the result of a constantly refined tradition. There are nearly a thousand years of history in this soup" (38).

The Authentic Piety of Mexican Converts

Yet Jean-Marie Latour is no gourmand living in scorn for his uncultured subjects. He is indeed drawn to the converted Mexicans who have embraced Christianity without abandoning their deep regard for the rhythms of the world. A good deal of paganism remains alive in these simple Christians, the Archbishop admits, especially in their fondness for the trinkets and trumpery of conventional religious practice—the amulets, for example, that seem magically to guarantee the fruitfulness of the fields. Latour patiently accommodates their wooden Virgins dressed as poor and sorrowful Mexican mothers, their St. Josephs attired as Mexican rancheros: They express the authentic piety of the people, not the imported spirituality of refined Europeans such as himself and Father Vaillant. Their churches seem "a part of the high colour that was in landscape and gardens, in the flaming cactus and gaudily decorated altars,—in the agonized Christs and dolorous Virgins and the very human figures of the saints. He had already learned that with this people religion was necessarily theatrical" (142). Latour is not troubled, therefore, that the nursery-like Madonnas serve the Mexican believers as both "their doll and their queen, something to fondle and something to adore, as Mary's Son must have been to Her":

> These poor Mexicans, he reflected, were not the first to pour out their love in this simple fashion. Raphael and Titian had made costumes for Her in their time, and the great masters had made music

> for Her, and the great architects had made cathedrals for Her. Long before Her years on earth, in the long twilight between the Fall and the Redemption, the pagan sculptors were always trying to achieve the image of a goddess who should yet be a woman. (257)

The sacraments of the Church prevent such popular devotional images and practices from degenerating into magic. Most of the Mexicans long for baptism and marriage because they have learned, if only in an inchoate way, that their lives are given ultimate direction and hope only as they receive what the natural world cannot give—the supernatural grace that puts them in right relation to God and thus to each other. Yet never does Cather depict the Archbishop or his vicar as anything other than ordinary parish priests doing their work. Even when, having been dispatched by Latour to administer the sacrament to dying Indians during an outbreak of black measles at Las Vegas, where Vaillant himself contracts the illness, Cather reports his heroic action as a mere matter of fact, not with hagiographic hyperbole.

Miracles as Violations or Deepenings of the Natural?

Naively pious Father Joseph believes that there in Las Vegas he had been divinely cured. With regard to the question of miracles, the two men stand at polar antipodes. Latour is a cultured Catholic who, in good Thomist fashion, interprets miracles as God's working within the contours of the universe, not invading them from without. "The Miracles of the Church," he explains to opaque Vaillant, "seem to me to rest not so much on voices or feelings or healing power coming suddenly near to us from afar off, but upon our perceptions being made finer, so that for a moment our eyes can see and ears hear what is there about us always" (50). Miracles disclose not so much what God rarely does as what God is always doing, even if the miraculous can be discerned only through faithful lenses. To invoke God's name whenever we are visited with life's unaccountable mercies is, for the Archbishop, to take the Lord's name in vain, to make it trite, devoid of true reverence.

Father Vaillant refuses such keen theological insight. He insists that miracles are not real unless, as Father Latour humorously explains, they are "very direct and spectacular, not with Nature, but against it. He would almost be able to tell the colour of the mantle Our Lady wore when She took the mare by the bridle back yonder among the junipers and led her out of the pathless sand-hills, as the angel led the ass on the Flight into Egypt" (29).

Father Vaillant as the Most Valiant of Priests

Cather's omniscient narrator clearly sympathizes with the Archbishop. Yet she will not permit her readers to think ill of Father Vaillant. On the contrary, he is far more successful than Latour in converting Indians. He is also as shrewd as he is holy. Encountering a Mexican who is overjoyed that, in blessing it, the priest has made his house "right with Heaven" (61), he wheedles him into giving him not one but both of his prized pearl-white mules, Contento and Angelica. Vaillant wants to ensure that Latour has proper mounts. The Archbishop doesn't seek to reconcile his vicar's contradictions; he not only accepts but embraces, even admires them:

> His Vicar was one of the most truly spiritual men he had ever known, though he was attached to many of the things of this world. Fond as he was of good eating and good drinking, he not only rigidly observed all the fasts of the Church, but he never complained about the scantiness of the fare on his long missionary journeys. . . . From a little feast that would make other men heavy and desirous of repose, Father Vaillant would rise up revived, and work for ten or twelve hours with that ardour and thoroughness which accomplished such lasting results. (225–26)

In many ways, Joseph Vaillant is the real hero of the narrative, most especially in his ingenious methods of missionizing. With almost comic originality he devises a stagecoach to transport the accoutrements of his priesthood far northward to Colorado, there to offer the Gospel to the masses of recently-arrived, often hard-hearted gold miners. So great are his gifts that Father Vaillant is eventually made archbishop of this vast diocese. At their final parting, therefore, Father Latour confesses the superiority of his companion:

> "Blanchet," [his nickname for Vaillant] said the Bishop rising, "you are a better man than I. You have been a greater harvester of souls, without pride and without shame—and I am always a little cold—un pedant, as you used to say. If hereafter we have stars in our crown, yours will be a constellation. Give me your blessing."
>
> He knelt, and Father Vaillant, having blessed him, knelt and was blessed in turn. They embraced each other for the past—for the future. (259–60)

Archbishop Latour as Both Courageous Churchman and Man of Doubt

This is hardly to say that the Archbishop lacks the courage to confront hard opposition, as becomes evident in his treatment of the thuggish Padre Martinez at Taos. He had ruled over northern New Mexico as a virtual dictator, in temporal no less than ecclesial affairs, before the arrival of Latour. He remains a local tyrant, fathering children on Mexican maidens at his pleasure. Paradoxically, he is also a bookish brute. When French-born, French-schooled Latour calls Martinez to account for his sexual sins, the swaggering lecher justifies them by quoting (and grossly misinterpreting) the Bishop of Hippo: "Celibacy may all be very well for the French clergy, but not for ours. St. Augustine himself says it is better not to go against nature. I find every evidence that in his old age he regretted having practised continence" (145). Hence his warning that the Archbishop should not seek to reform the Indians by imposing European doctrines and practices. He cautions Latour not "to interfere with the secret dances of the Indians . . . or abolish the bloody rites of the Penitentes. I foretell an early death for you" (147).

Yet Cather refuses to turn Padre Martinez into the obvious antithesis of Latour. On the contrary, the corrupt cleric is a man of quality. He sings the Mass, for example, with an impressive baritone voice and deep devotional piety: "At the moment of the Elevation the dark priest seemed to give whole force, his swarthy body and all its blood, to that lifting up. Rightly guided, the Bishop reflected, the Mexican might have been a great man. He had an altogether compelling personality, a disturbing, mysterious, magnetic power" (150). Yet it is controlling power, *libido dominandi*, that matters most to Martinez. He dominates Lucero his student and *protégé* as a lackey at best, as a dumb beast at worst. Yet he finally ordains Lucero and makes him his vicar, as they form a schismatic church of their own. After they have ignored four solemn warnings against such heresy, the archbishop excommunicates them.[15] Far from being one who leaves

[15] As is often the case with Cather, she abandons few souls to utter damnation. In a complex series of extraneous episodes, we learn that dying Padre Lucero—who in the meantime had become a wretched miser and had even knifed a potential robber to death—seeks reconciliation with the Church. Father Vaillant quite valiantly rides to his rescue, in the thick of the night and at great personal danger, to shrive the dying Lucero. His salvation happily restored at last, Lucero nonetheless dies an unhappy death. In a deathbed vision, he beholds Padre Martinez in hellish torment.

the hardest tasks to Father Vaillant, Father Latour has a towering, steely bravery of his own.

The archbishop's fiercest struggle proves to be inward rather than outward. After more than two decades of service in New Mexico, and with only minimal success to show for it, Latour faces his *noche oscura*, as St. John of the Cross called it, his dark night of soul, a massive sense of spiritual emptiness and vocational failure: "His work seemed superficial, a house built upon the sands. His great diocese was still a heathen country. The Indians travelled their old road of fear and darkness, battling with evil omens and ancient shadows. The Mexicans were children who played with their religion" (211). Latour overcomes his *acedia* not in a solitary mental wrestling with God but in a communal encounter with an old Mexican woman named Sada.

A Marian Answer to Spiritual Despair

Though enslaved to a family of viciously anti-Catholic Protestants for nineteen years, Sada has courageously fled at last to the sacristy of the Church to seek solace. Leading the weeping woman into the Lady Chapel, the Archbishop kneels and prays with her, knowing that her tears spring from ecstasy far more than sorrow. For Latour to have comforted this solitary sufferer whose life remains utterly negligible according the world's measure is for him to have recovered far more than his own personal faith; he has also rediscovered the absolute indispensability of the Church and its sacraments, its prayers and vigils, its saints and martyrs, for human existence to remain human:

> Never, as he afterward told Father Vaillant, had it been permitted him to behold such deep experience of the holy joy of religion as on that pale December night. He was able to feel, kneeling beside her, the preciousness of the things of the altar to her who was without possessions; the tapers, the image of the Virgin, the figures of the saints, the Cross that took away indignity from suffering and made pain and poverty a means of fellowship with Christ. Kneeling beside the much enduring bond-woman, he experienced those holy mysteries as he had done in his young manhood. . . .

Rather than pitying the damned man, Lucero bursts forth with a final serpentine curse: "'Comete tu cola, Martinez, comete tu cola! (Eat your tail, Martinez, eat your tail!)'" (171). It is evident, though the narrator does not say so, that Padre Lucero will require a considerable stay in Purgatory to heal his vengeful hatred.

> Not often, indeed, had Jean-Marie Latour come so near to the Fountain of all Pity as in the Lady Chapel that night; the pity that no man born of woman could ever utterly cut himself off from; [the Pity] that was for the murderer on the scaffold, as it was for the dying soldier or the martyr on the rack. (217–18)

Perhaps because she was a high-church Episcopalian, Cather gives this Pity an unapologetically Marian and Catholic quality. It is not enough, therefore, that the Archbishop promises to "remember [Sada] in my silent supplications before the altar as I do my own sisters and nieces" (217); he must also offer the Blessed Sacrifice of the Mass, as he calls it, in his pro-cathedra[16] whose very edifice makes proper tribute to the Son and Mother of God.

A Cathedral Meant to Glorify the Gospel in Stone

Yet the Archbishop's ultimate ambition is to build a *real* cathedral. Though it need not be a replica of European models, neither can it exist in utter disregard for the achievements of Christendom. And so Latour yearns for a properly Romanesque Church—not a fancy Gothic structure of the kind being constructed in Victorian England, but a sanctuary that would link the Church of the New World more directly with the Roman world from which the ancient Church first emerged. When he at last discovers the native rock from which the cathedral stones can be quarried, the Archbishop experiences a veritable epiphany: "Every time I come here, I like this stone better. I could have hardly hoped that God would gratify my personal taste, my vanity, if you will, in this way. I tell you, Blanchet, I would rather have found this hill of yellow rock than have come into a fortune to spend in charity. The Cathedral is near my heart, for many reasons. I hope you do not think me very worldly" (245).

Despite the secular irrelevance of this future sanctuary, despite the princely sums it will cost that might have been better used to succor the poor, despite the many decades required to complete it, and then decades more for it to become thoroughly at one with the ethos of Santa Fé—such objections are nothing to the point. Unlike the European cookery and gardens and orchards that Latour and Vaillant value so highly, the cathedral will stand not chiefly as a magnificent aesthetic edifice but rather as

16 A temporary cathedral used by a bishop until a more permanent or suitable church is built.

a wondrous architectural embodiment of the Gospel. Christ's Church, Cather insists, provides no gnostic escape for discarnate spirits; it offers divine deliverance for ensouled bodies. They require a stonework witness pointing to the God who has made himself visible by tabernacling in the world through his Son and his Church and its sacraments.

Dying not from Disease but from Having Lived

It is altogether fitting that Latour should die not at the rural retreat where he had retired but in the shadow of his familiar makeshift cathedral—not amid the haunting silence of the natural world but within the quiet stir of the Church. As he takes leave of the past, the aged archbishop thinks less and less of his beloved Clermont in France, recognizing instead that Christians are meant to dwell in perpetual exile, living as resident aliens with no permanent citizenship in any other City than the one not made with hands. Neither is the dying priest vexed by worries over the future. Everything temporal has begun to merge into a single moment of memory and vision: "He was soon to have done with calendared time, and it had already ceased to count for him. He sat in the middle of his own consciousness; none of his former states of mind were lost or outgrown. They were all within reach of his hand, and all comprehensible" (288).

Though he wishes Father Vaillant were present for his earthly exit, Father Latour is content to die alone amidst what he calls the "solitariness of love in which a priest's life could be like his Master's. It was not a solitude of atrophy, of negation, but of perpetual flowering" (254). At the end, the Archbishop makes perhaps the most blessed death in all of American literature, not so much because he dies in peaceful gratitude for the partial fulfillment of his mission, but rather because his whole life has readied him for his death. Such a *preparatio mori* is not, for Christians, the same thing that Socrates calls for in Plato's Apology. It is a matter of the priest's having rightly ordered his loves, and thus having brought his life to its true completion. In final obedience to the Dominical command to "Be perfect, therefore, as your heavenly Father is perfect" (Matt 5:48), Jean-Marie Latour has made his life all the way through in the root sense of the word *perficere*. The waning Archbishop thus announces—with sudden and surprising strength, and in what may be the book's signature sentence—that "I shall not die of a cold. . . . I shall die of having lived" (267).

The final perfecting of Jean-Marie Latour's life accomplishes not his salvation alone but also that of his entire community. The Archbishop has been formed by the Church for the sake of the Church. It was not only the Mexicans of Santa Fé who fell on their knees at the tolling of Jean-Marie Latour's death bell, therefore, but "all American Catholics as well" (299). The narrator might well have said "all American Christians as well," for Willa Cather's *Death Comes for the Archbishop* remains the most singular work of American literature wherein the Church, though nearly everywhere else blocked from our vision, clearly and redemptively emerges.

The Figure of Augusta in *The Professor's House*

The Professor's House is one of Willa Cather's most accomplished novels. It is a highly nuanced account of a highly accomplished professor who has written an eight-volume history of medieval Spain. Professor St. Peter lives his scholarly life in a somewhat dilapidated house near Lake Michigan in an Illinois town where his university is located. His story is set during the early Prohibition years of the 1920s. Godfrey St. Peter is a contradictory character. He is so thoroughly devoted to his academic work, for instance, that he often neglects his wife and two daughters. Nor is he a paragon of moral purity. Erotic attractions are never far removed from his mind, as he transfers them even to the mannikins used by a fellow occupant of the house, Augusta the seamstress, whose surname we never learn. He refers to her wooden models as "my ladies," though he never offers any sexual overtures to devout Augusta.

We first meet her as she is returning from Mass. Immediately she becomes associated with things generally Catholic and specifically Marian: the Mystical Rose, the Lily of Zion, the Magnificat.[17] Godfrey St. Peter has at least heard of the Magnificat, but when Augusta tells him that it doesn't describe the Blessed Virgin's attributes but consists of her own faithful hymn in response to Gabriel's Annunciation, he hilariously assumes that it must be her own artistic composition, like any other well-known musical work:

> Augusta spoke gently, as if she were prompting him and did not wish to rebuke his ignorance too sharply. "Why, yes, just as soon as the angel announced to her that she would be the mother of our Lord, the Blessed Virgin composed the Magnificat. I always think of you as knowing everything, Doctor St. Peter!"

[17] It may not be too far-fetched to imagine her as a Marian figure in her own way.

"And you're always finding out how little I know," [he replies]. "Well don't give me away. You are very discreet."[18]

An Ordinary Death Made Extraordinary

When, at the novel's end, the professor comes to his own ending, Augusta doesn't "give him away" but discreetly shrives his soul. Having collapsed in his study back at the old house where he had found his most productive scholarly life, he finds only Augusta there to succor him. No longer does he regard her as a simple-minded seamstress who selflessly attended to the needy but rather as the true and full human being whom he is not:

> Augusta, he reflected, had always been a corrective, a remedial influence. . . . She came early, often directly from church, and had her breakfast with the Professor, before the rest of the family were up. Very often she gave him some wise observation or discreet comment to begin the day with. She wasn't afraid to say things that were heavily, drearily true, and though he used to wince under them, he hurried off with the feeling that they were good for him, that he didn't have to hear such things often enough. Augusta was like the taste of bitter herbs; she was the bloomless side of life that he had always run away from,—yet when he had to face it, he found that it wasn't altogether repugnant. (255–56)

Far from finding her repugnant, the otherwise opaque Godfrey learns to honor Augusta's unflustered regard for death, as yet again Cather draws on the Golden Legend. In an interview, Cather reported that "in the Golden Legend the martyrdoms of the saints are no more dwelt upon than are the trivial incidents of their lives; it is as though all human experiences, measured against one supreme spiritual experience, were of about the same importance."[19] Hence Professor St. Peters' thankful admission that Augusta "hadn't any of the sentimentality that comes from the fear of dying. She talked about death as she spoke of a hard winter or a rainy March, or any of the sadnesses of nature" (256). "Theoretically," he adds, "he knew that life is possible, may be even pleasant, without joy, without passionate griefs. But it had never occurred to him that he might have to live like that" (257).

18 Willa Cather, *The Professor's House* (New York, Vintage, 1990 [1925]), 84. Further references to the novel will be paginated within the text.

19 Cather, *On Writing*, 5.

Not, of course, that passionate delights and sorrows are negligible; exactly to the contrary, they are the very stuff of life. Yet when such penultimate things become ultimate, they fail finally to satisfy, leading to final grief. That Godfrey St. Peter comes to live without dependence on them, if only in his last moments, may be worth an eternity. That he learns this ultimate truth from a faithful Catholic seamstress makes it all the more remarkable.[20]

[20] Tom Haddox, my companion in first and final things, not only encouraged me to consider the excellences of *The Professor's House* but also, far more significantly, to grasp the profound Catholic witness of Augusta.

3

Flannery O'Connor's Catholic Priests and Protestant Preachers

Stanley Hauerwas insists that the churches' restored visibility in our time and place will entail "a confidence in our most basic acts that make us the Church of Jesus Christ—that is, the preaching of the word as true and the celebration of the Eucharist [as real]. It is the preaching of Christ and the celebration of his crucifixion and resurrection that [as] Bonhoeffer rightly reminded us makes possible lives that can identify the lies that threaten our lives."[1] Eucharistic images and moments appear throughout Flannery O'Connor's fiction, especially in *The Violent Bear It Away*, where the sacramentally starved Rayber pauses hungrily but also unbelievingly before a loaf of bread in a bakery window. Yet for my purposes, it is O'Connor's uncompromising priests and preachers—as embodiments and proclaimers of the Word—who also call for scrutiny.

There is not a whiff of Catholic triumphalism in Flannery O'Connor's work. Never does she suggest that Rome is right and everyone else is wrong.[2] On the contrary, she repeatedly laments the gross failure of her own Communion. "If you live today," she declared in 1955, "you breathe in nihilism. In or out of the Church, it's the gas you breathe" (HB, 97). This is a crucial admission since, as we shall see, "nihilism" is another word for the demonic. O'Connor was so fearful of being dismissed as a

1 Stanley Hauerwas, "The Challenge for Christian Ministry at the End of Christendom," *ABC Religion and Ethics*, July 14, 2017, updated January 10, 2019, https://www.abc.net.au/religion/why-bonhoeffer-matters-the-challenge-for-christian-ministry-at-t/10095618.

2 Though her death in 1964 occurred before the Second Vatican Council's Decree on Ecumenism, she would surely have approved its declaration that Protestants are no longer to be regarded as heretics (i.e., non-Christians) but as "separated brethren."

Catholic triumphalist—especially with her hyper-Irish name, Mary Flannery O'Connor!—that she gives a full portrait of only two priests in her stories. They offer completely contrasting versions of the Church as it is made visible, and they both appear in one of her last and finest stories, "The Enduring Chill."

Father Vogle and Father Finn

Asbury Fox is a failed New York writer who has returned home to die, he thinks, as a martyr to his mother's smothering ruin of his artistic talents. Fox is not nearly as cunning as his name seems to suggest, for he is suffering from the serious though not deadly disease of undulant fever. He had contracted it while attempting a secular communion with two black workers whom he urged to join him in drinking freely of the dairy's readily available milk. These shrewd farm hands knew, of course, that unpasteurized milk can carry Bang's disease from cows to humans. And so they cunningly abstained.

Believing that he is imminently dying when he is in fact lastingly alive, Asbury insists that his mother summon not a local Methodist pastor but a Catholic priest to his death bed. He knows exactly the kind of cleric who will treat him as he wishes: Ignatius Vogle, S.J. Fox had encountered Vogle at a meeting of Asbury's New York friends as they were celebrating their faux-Hindu religion: "Salvation," quoted their leader Goetz, "is the destruction of a simple prejudice, and no one is saved." Asbury was drawn to Vogle because he is "a man of the world." The priest had observed these assembled sophisticates with a "polite but strictly reserved interest" and a "taciturn superior expression." When Asbury asks the Jesuit to answer Goetz's cool nihilism, Vogle voices abstractions whose distanced adverbial tone appeals to sophisticated Asbury. "'There is a real probability of the New Man, assisted, of course,' he added brittlely, 'by the Third Person of the Trinity.' 'Ridiculous!' the girl in the sari said, but the priest only brushed her with his smile, which was slightly amused now" (CW, 550).

Needless to say, no such cultured Jesuit is to be found in a small Southern town. Mrs. Fox locates what she hopes will be a suitable substitute: Father Finn. This elderly, half-deaf, thoroughly uncultured priest with a quintessential Irish name seems an easy target for Asbury's acid wit. Alas for Asbury, it proves not to be so, as becomes evident in a rollicking non-exchange worth quoting in full:

The priest lifted his chair and pushed closer. "You'll have to shout," he said. "Blind in one eye and deaf in one ear."

"What do you think of Joyce?" Asbury said louder.

"Joyce? Joyce who?" asked the priest.

"James Joyce," Asbury said and laughed.

The priest brushed his huge hand in the air as if he were bothered by gnats. "I haven't met him," he said. "Now. Do you say your morning and your night prayers?"

Asbury appeared confused. "Joyce was a great writer," he murmured, forgetting to shout.

"You don't, eh?" said the priest. "Well you will never learn to be good unless you pray regularly. You cannot love Jesus unless you speak to Him."

"The myth of the dying god had always fascinated me," Asbury shouted, but the priest did not appear to catch it.

"Do you have trouble with purity?" he demanded, and as Asbury paled, he went on without waiting for an answer. "We all do but we must pray to the Holy Ghost for it. Mind, heart and body. Nothing is overcome without prayer. . . ."

"The artist prays by creating," Asbury ventured.

"Not enough!" snapped the priest. "If you do not pray daily you are neglecting your immortal soul. Do you know your catechism?"

"Certainly not," Asbury muttered.

"Who made you?" the priest asked in a martial tone.

"Different people believe different things about that," Asbury said.

"God made you," the priest said shortly. "Who is God?"

"God is an idea created by man," Asbury said, feeling that he was getting into his stride, that two could play at this.

"God is a spirit infinitely perfect," the priest said. "You are a very ignorant boy. Why did God make you?"

"God didn't. . . ."

"God made you to know Him, to love Him, to serve Him in this world and to be happy with Him in the next!" the old priest said with a battering voice. "If you don't apply yourself to the catechism how do you expect to know how to save your immortal soul? . . . Do you want your soul to suffer eternal damnation? Do you want to be deprived of God for all eternity? Do you want to suffer the most terrible pain, greater than fire, the pain of loss? Do you want to suffer the pain of loss for all eternity?" (CW, 565–67)

In Bakhtinian terms, Father Finn is not a benignly dialogical but a mischievously monological priest. Yet O'Connor virtually dares her readers to dismiss him as a reactionary throwback to a bygone time. His grilling of Asbury Fox is taken straight from the Baltimore Catechism, the standard text used in U.S. Catholic churches and schools from 1885 through the late 1960s. It enables Father Finn to strike straight at the heart of the matter, telling arrogant Asbury what he most needs but least wants to hear. Yet Father Finn is no cold-souled priest. He has a true pastoral heart. He doesn't accuse Asbury of mortal but of venial sin: vincible ignorance. There is still time for him to learn the basic teachings of the Church. "The poor lad doesn't even know his catechism," he declares to Mrs. Fox. Hence Father Finn's final words to her: "He's a good lad at heart but very ignorant" (CW, 567).

The old priest's estimate of Asbury is validated at the story's end when the sick but surviving youth is made to face the freezing truth about himself. There, as he looks up in horror at a bird-like stain on the ceiling, the Third Person plunges down upon him: "The last film of illusion was torn as by a whirlwind from his eyes. He saw that for the rest of his days, frail, racked, but enduring, he would live in the face of a purifying terror. A feeble cry, a last impossible protest escaped him. But the Holy Ghost, emblazoned in ice rather than fire continued, implacable, to descend" (CW, 572).

Hazel Motes as Preacher of a Placeless Gospel

Flannery O'Connor had no fear of giving full voice to the proclamation of the nihilist word. In *Wise Blood* she portrays Hazel Motes as pastor and sole member of the Church Without Christ. He is a twenty-two-year-old veteran returning to his Tennessee home from the Second War, not to make a new life for himself, but to repudiate the Gospel his evangelist-grandfather had aimed directly at him:

> They were like stones! [the elderly preacher] would shout. But Jesus had died to redeem them! Jesus was so soul-hungry that He had died, one death for all, but He would have died every soul's death for one! Did they understand that? Did they understand that for each stone soul, He would have died ten million deaths, had his arms and legs stretched on a cross and nailed ten million times for one of them? (The old man would point to his grandson Haze.) . . . Did they know that even for that boy there, that mean, sinful, unthinking boy stand-

ing there with his dirty hands . . . Jesus would die ten million deaths before He would let him lose his soul? He would chase him over the waters of sin! Did they doubt that Jesus could walk on the waters of sin? That boy had been redeemed and . . . Jesus would never let him forget he was redeemed. What did the sinner think was to be gained? Jesus would have him in the end! (CW, 10–11)

Wise Blood—O'Connor's remarkable first sustained work of fiction, published when she was but twenty-seven—is a complex account of Motes' angry flight from the Hound of Heaven. As a proclaimer of a nihilist gospel, he brings it to clearest focus in a sermon where, with keen authorial irony, O'Connor has Motes identify the chief rubrics of the Faith even as he repudiates them:

"I preach there are all kinds of truth, your truth and somebody else's, but behind all of them there is only one truth and that is that there's no truth," he called. "No truth behind all truths is what I and this church preach! Where you come from is gone, where you thought you were going to never was there, and where you are is no good unless you can get away from it. Where is there a place for you to be? No place.

"Nothing outside can give you any place," he said. "You needn't look to the sky because it's not going to open and show no place behind it. You needn't to search for any hole in the ground to look through into somewhere else. You can't go neither forwards nor backwards into your daddy's time nor your children's if you have them. In yourself right now is all the place you've got. If there was any Fall, look there, if there was any Redemption, look there, and if you expect any Judgment, look there, because they all three will have to be in your time and your body and where in your time and your body can they be?" (CW, 93)

It would be all too easy to lynch Motes in the rope of his own illogic; for, if the truth is that there is no truth, then his own claims are also untrue. Far better, I believe, to deal with Haze's obsession with place, since the novel is redolent with references to the word. This first becomes evident when Motes returns from the war to his rural village of Eastrod, only to find that his home is all but gone: "Though he saw that the fence around it had partly fallen and that weeds were growing through the porch floor, he didn't realize all at once that it was only a shell, that there was nothing here but the skeleton of a house." Thieves had taken every item except the walnut chifforobe in the kitchen where his mother slept. "He took the wrapping cord and tied it around the legs and through the floor boards and left a piece of paper in each of the drawers: THIS SHIFFER-ROBE BELONGS TO HAZEL MOTES. DO NOT STEAL IT OR YOU WILL BE HUNTED DOWN AND KILLED" (CW, 13–14).

What may seem to be Motes' negligible loss is a weighty matter instead. Human beings cannot flourish without a sense of place, a rootage in concrete times and locations that give ontological significance to their lives. I do not use this forbidding word lightly. As Jordan Rowan Fannin observes,

> To be in the presence of that which I did not make . . . confronts me simply by its existence. What O'Connor grasps is the simple yet profound truth that its existence is what makes it ontologically significant. . . . Being confronted with the ontological reality or beingness of the world does not signify the world's independence . . . but its givenness. The givenness of the world changes its meaning considerably, shifting the accent from the world's separateness from humans to the possibility of our intimacy with it. . . . Its existence confronts me as a kind of limit—as that which does not depend on me for its existence and, therefore, escapes in some prior sense my power and my will. Yet, O'Connor recognizes that at one and the same time, this limit is the very moment of possibility. In this act of confrontation, all that is not-me opens up the grand possibility that my existence is not a task but a response. The recognition that the world is not of my own making can create an openness to the ways in which both the world and the self are not made but created, not established but gifted, not works of immanent agency but signs of divine agency and act.[3]

In Walker Percy's *The Moviegoer*, his novel of 1961, the narrator/protagonist Binx Bolling puts a similar stress on the important of place, as he recalls a childhood trip with his father to Chicago:

> Not a single thing do I remember from the first trip but this: the sense of the place, the savor of the genie-soul of the place which every place has or else is not a place. I could have been wrong: it could have been

[3] Jordan Rowan Fannin, "Following Flannery, Locating Ourselves: The Theological Significance of Place in Flannery O'Connor" (PhD diss., Baylor University, 2016), 76–77.

> nothing of the sort, not the memory of a place but the memory of being a child. But one step out into the brilliant March day and there it is as big as life, the genie-soul of the place which, wherever you go, you must meet and master first thing or be met and mastered. . . . Nobody but a Southerner knows the wrenching rinsing sadness of the cities of the North. Knowing all about genie-souls and living in haunted places like Shiloh and the Wilderness and Vicksburg and Atlanta where the ghosts of heroes walk abroad by day and are more real than people, he knows a ghost when he sees one, and no sooner does he step off the train in New York or Chicago or San Francisco than he feels the genie-soul perched on his shoulder.[4]

For Walker Percy as for Binx Bolling, not to possess a sense of place is to be an anybody dwelling anywhere and thus a nobody dwelling nowhere—a fate that Hazel Motes rightly fears and dreads. As Peter Candler explains, "Specific places, specific feelings—related to our memories of the place, perhaps, or to some quality of unexpected newness that we don't experience in the place we call home . . . generate specific thoughts, concepts: ideas that do not occur to us anywhere else."[5] They lay claims on us, as we in turn confess our obligations to them. In the generic sense, "places" may have no geographical locale; they may be as airy as the ethos of one's childhood hometown, though it is now dilapidated, or as specific as the smell of hickory-wood smoke or the taste of fried okra. Yet the effect is the same: Such places recall us to unexpected newness and oblige us to fulfill neglected duties.

Hazel Motes hammers the impossibility of place for obvious reasons. He is fleeing such unexpected newness, such abandoned duty. Having lost all rootage in the transcendent realm of givenness and openness, Motes preaches a gospel with a negative *telos*. As Julia Hejduk explains, this is a philosophical impossibility:

> *Telos* means what something is for, the ultimate end at which it aims. The telos of an acorn is to be an oak tree. The telos of a human community is to enable the flourishing of its members, and ultimately of

[4] Walker Percy, *The Moviegoer* (New York: Noonday, 1967), 202–3.

[5] See the June 11, 2023, installment of Candler's blog, *The Detourist*, https://adeepersouth.substack.com/p/homecoming-2023. Such keen perceptions permeate both of Candler's recent books: *The Road to Unforgetting: Detours in the American South, 1997–2022* (Durham, N.C.: Horse and Buggy Press, 2023) and *A Deeper South: The Beauty, Mystery and Sorrow of the Southern Road* (Columbia: University of South Carolina Press, 2024).

> the whole human family. Christianity maintains that the telos of a human being is to share forever in the divine life of the triune God, who is the primordial community of Love. By definition, a *telos* must be a positive goal.[6]

It should come as no surprise that Motes' impossible negative teleology ends in murderous violence. As Hejduk explains, "Any negative *telos* can be accomplished most completely through an atrocity. One can effectively stop [others] from acting in a certain way by imposing forcible restrictions on their behavior. . . . In the most extreme case, human evils can be eradicated by eradicating the humans who perpetrate them." Thus does Hazel Motes end by murdering Solace Layfield in a failed attempt to deny his ultimate emplacement.

Hazel Motes as Self-Mutilating Protestant Saint

Having recently encountered Sophocles' *Oedipus the King* in Robert Fitzgerald's translation, Flannery O'Connor ended *Wise Blood* by having Hazel Motes undertake a grotesque penance for untruthfully preaching and murderously enacting his nihilist gospel that nothing is true but one's own body and place. The only life Motes knows is flight. His home and nearly all other tangible signs of his original place are lost. He thus searches for such signs—of Fall, Redemption, Judgment—in himself, in his own body. Precisely there must he work out his salvation: by mutilating the flesh he once deified. Thus does he put bits of broken glass in his shoes, bind his chest with barbed wire, and finally blind himself with quicklime. As he explains to Mrs. Flood, his uncomprehending landlady, "If there's no bottom in your eyes, they hold more" (CW, 126).

While O'Connor declared that only such a Roman Catholic as herself could have written such a novel as *Wise Blood*, she was also careful to call Motes a Protestant saint. He is clearly the hero of her novel, whom she portrays with the utmost sympathy. He is one of her folk-Christian heroes[7] with whom she was profoundly agreed about the nature of sin and the necessity of redemption. Even so, she lamented their failure to

6 Julia D. Hejduk, "You Can't Have a *Telos* of No," *Christian Scholars Review*, April 19, 2023, https://christianscholars.com/you-cant-have-a-telos-of-no/.

7 It is not quite right to describe O'Connor's backwoods believers as fundamentalists. Fundamentalism was not primarily a Southern and rural but rather a Northern and urban phenomenon. It sprang up in Chicago and Minneapolis, largely in response to a religious crisis over evolution during the 1920s. When modern

regard the Church as the necessary means of salvation: "The religion of the South is a do-it-yourself religion, something which I as a Catholic find painful and touching and grimly comic. It is full of unconscious pride that lands them in all sorts of ridiculous religious predicaments. They have nothing to correct their practical heresies and so they work them out dramatically" (CW, 1107). Having denied the ontological reality that could have grounded him in time and space, Motes manufactures his own negative religion with its negative *telos*. And when it fails, he remakes himself into a pseudo *sacerdos* in an act of self-mutilation that magisterial Catholic teaching forbids and condemns.[8] With no recourse to such higher ecclesial authority, Motes immolates himself in macabre fashion. That he is the novel's heroic saint is without question, even if he remains an heretically Protestant one.

---

scientists began to posit an old-fashioned, closed, and inerrant universe, these biblicists posited, over against it, a new-fashioned, closed, and inerrant Bible.

As John Hayes has shown, Flannery O'Connor's shotgun-wielding prophets and baptizing river preachers are nothing of this sort. They embody, instead, the 1950s folk Christianity of poor and emarginated Southerners, black and white alike. They've never heard of the alleged inerrant autographs. Far from being fixated on such small-minded matters, they wrestle with the Bible as if tangling with a wildcat. Abraham's sword hangs over their heads. Their Jesus walks on the waters of sin. Both to their terror and their hope, they have ears to hear and eyes to see (John Hayes, *Hard, Hard Religion: Interracial Faith in the Poor South* [Chapel Hill: University of North Carolina Press, 2017]).

8 "Except when performed for strictly therapeutic medical reasons, directly intended amputations, mutilations, and sterilizations . . . are against the moral law" (*Catechism of the Catholic Church*, 2nd ed., para. 2297).

> Reacting to a report that Pope John Paul II practiced self-mortification, including flagellation, experts in spirituality said ascetical practices are part of the Christian tradition, but should be used in moderation and under the guidance of a mature spiritual director.
>
> "Union with the redeeming suffering of Christ comes through accepting the trials and suffering of life or, like in the case of Pope John Paul II, with the voluntary choice of physical suffering," said Cardinal Georges Cottier, theologian of the papal household under the late pope.
>
> "Spiritual masters insist this practice must always be prudent and never without a spiritual guide," because "pathological abuses are always possible," the cardinal said . . . in a written response to questions from Catholic News Service. Cardinal Cottier said the practice of self-mortification did not conflict with what Pope John Paul wrote and preached about the beauty and sacredness of the human body and the obligation of Christians to care for their bodies.

National Catholic Reporter, "Self-mortification Must Be Moderate, Monitored," February 5, 2010, https://www.ncronline.org/news/vatican/self-mortification-must-be-moderate-monitored.

Bevel Summers as River-Preacher of the Blood of Christ

I am far from suggesting that O'Connor treats all of her Protestant preachers as sub-Catholic and thus quasi-heretical. Two notable counterexamples are found in Bevel Summers in "The River" and Lucette Carmody in *The Violent Bear It Away*—perhaps because they are both too young to have landed in what O'Connor called "ridiculous religious predicaments."

As a preacher in his late teens, Summers has no pulpit of his own. He proclaims the Word while standing in a shallow stream, beckoning to all who will hear and heed his proclamation. Baptism for him is no affirmation of one's individual promise to follow Jesus. Though untutored in sacramental theology, he has a sacramental regard for baptism as the outward and visible act of initiation of believers into death and burial with Christ, as they then rise up out of their watery grave to drastic newness of life.

As a one who also has the gift of healing, Summers worries that his audience may have come either to witness or perhaps even to receive a sensational cure. He promises no such miraculous relief but unspectacular healing instead—i.e., a transformation that makes witness to the Gospel: "If you ain't come for Jesus, you ain't come for me. If you just come to see can you leave your pain in the river, you ain't come for Jesus . . . I never told nobody that" (CW, 162). Bevel thus makes clear that there are two kinds of pain and two sorts of rivers, both spiritual and physical:

> Then he lifted his head and arms and shouted. "Listen to what I got to say, you people! There ain't but one river and that's the River of Life, made out of Jesus' Blood. That's the river you have to lay your pain in, in the River of Faith, in the River of Life, in the River of Love, in the rich red river of Jesus' Blood, you people!"
>
> His voice grew soft and musical. "All the rivers come from that one River and go back to it like it was the ocean sea and if you believe, you can lay your pain in that River and get rid of it because that's the River that was made to carry sin. It's a River full of pain itself, pain itself, moving toward the Kingdom of Christ, to be washed away, *slow*, you people, *slow* as this here old red river water round my feet." (CW, 162; emphasis added)[9]

[9] If Summers were to call for his faithful river-congregation to sing, they would surely have burst forth with this Gospel song from my Baptist boyhood: "What can wash away my sin? / Nothing but the blood of Jesus. / What can make me

Though he lacks formal theological training, Bevel Summers has saturated his theological imagination in the doctrine of Substitutionary Atonement. Though subject to gross abuse, it is rightly understood as measuring the cost of divine forgiveness—both the cost to Christ and the cost to his disciples. Note well that the river-evangelist does not call for an instantaneous, once-for-all conversion to the cheap grace denounced by Dietrich Bonhoeffer:

> Grace without price; grace without cost! The essence of grace, we suppose, is that the account has been paid in advance; and, because it has been paid, everything can be had for nothing. Since the cost was infinite, the possibilities of using and spending it are infinite. What would grace be if it were not cheap?
>
> Grace alone does everything, they say, and so everything can remain as it was before. Instead of following Christ, let the Christian enjoy the consolations of grace! That is what we mean by cheap grace, the grace which amounts to the justification of sin without the justification of the repentant sinner who departs from sin and from whom sin departs. Cheap grace is the grace we bestow on ourselves.[10]

Instead, Bevel Summers summons his flock to costly grace—the hard, *slow*, muddy struggle of daily reconversion to the life of radical discipleship:

> Such grace is costly because it calls us to follow, and it is grace because it calls us to follow Jesus Christ. It is costly because it costs a man his life, and it is grace because it gives a man the only true life. It is costly because it condemns sin, and grace because it justifies the sinner. Above all, it is costly because it cost God the life of His Son: "Ye were bought at a price" (1 Cor. 6:20), and what has cost God much cannot be cheap for us. Costly grace is the incarnation of God.
>
> Grace is costly because it compels a man to submit to the yoke of Christ and follow him; it is grace because Jesus says: "My yoke is easy and my burden is light" (Mt. 11:30).[11]

---

whole again? / Nothing but the blood of Jesus. / Oh! precious is the flow, / that makes me white as snow, / no other fount I know, / nothing but the blood of Jesus."

10 Dietrich Bonhoeffer, *Dietrich Bonhoeffer Works*, vol. 4, *Discipleship*, ed. Martin Kuske and Ilse Tödt, English trans. ed. Geffrey B. Kelly and John D. Godsey (Minneapolis: Fortress, 2001), 43.

11 Bonhoeffer, *Discipleship*, 43.

Lucette Carmody as Truthful Proclaimer of God's Burning Word

Far and away the most powerful sermon in Flannery O'Connor's fiction comes from a child evangelist named Lucette Carmody in *The Violent Bear It Away*. The parents of this well-named "little light" have fitted her out with a cape flamboyantly flung over her shoulder, though it doesn't disguise her deformity—"the thin legs twisted from the knees." Lucette's sermon, far from being a laughable "carmody," requires full explication, since it is surely the strongest in American literature:

> "I want to tell you people the story of the world," she said in a loud high child's voice. "I want to tell you why Jesus came and what happened to Him. I want to tell you how He'll come again. I want to tell you to be ready. Most of all," she said, "I want to tell you to be ready, so that on the last day you'll rise in the glory of the Lord. . . ."
>
> "Do you know who Jesus is?" she cried. "Jesus is the Word of God and Jesus is love. The Word of God is love and do you know what love is, you people? If you don't know what love is you won't know Jesus when He comes. You won't be ready." (CW, 411–12)

Though little Miss Carmody pronounces an apocalyptic word of admonition, hers is not chiefly a warning about the wrath to come. Her main concern is to recount the world's true story, in the sense specified by Robert Jenson:

> The story the Bible tells is asserted to be the story of God with His creatures; that is, it is both assumed and explicitly asserted that there is a true story about the universe because there is a universal novelist/historian. . . . But this is precisely what the postmodern church cannot presume. What then? The obvious answer is that if the church does not find her hearers antecedently inhabiting a narratable world, then the church must herself be that world. . . . The church has in fact had great experience of just this role. One of many analogies between postmodernity and dying antiquity—in which the church lived for her most creative period—is that the late antique world also insisted on being a meaningless chaos, and that the church had to save her converts by offering herself as the narratable world within which life could be lived with dramatic

> coherence. Israel had been the nation that lived a realistic narrative amid nations that lived otherwise.[12]

Lucette Carmody proceeds to tell the true story of the world's Fall, of God's promised Redemption of it, but also of the world's romantic desire for a triumphant King who would come in astonishing glory in order to rule in obvious wonder and delight:

> "Listen to me, you people," she said. "God was angry with the world because it always wanted more. It wanted as much as God had and it didn't know what God had but it wanted it and more. It wanted God's own breath, it wanted His very Word, and God said, 'I'll make my Word Jesus, I'll give them my Word for a king. I'll give my very breath for theirs.'
>
> "Listen you people," she said and flung her arms wide, "God told the world He was going to send it a king and the world waited. The world thought, a golden fleece will do for His bed. Silver and gold and peacock tails, a thousand suns in a peacock's tail will do for His sash. His mother will ride on a four-horned white beast and use the sunset for a cape. She'll trail it behind her over the ground and let the world pull it to pieces, a new one every evening. . . ."
>
> "The world said, 'How long, Lord, do we have to wait for this?' And the Lord said, 'My Word is coming from the house of David, the king.'" (CW, 412)

Then follows Lucette's stunning peroration. There she sets forth the stark gap between a lovely affection that would leave humanity dead in its sins and trespasses over against the plain saving Love who was born in a cowstall to a young Jewish virgin. She and her Child were in turn forced to flee the massacring Jewish accomplice of Roman tyranny, even as her own heart would also be pierced when the human mob eventually crucified her Son, though they knew not what they had done.

> She began in a dirge-like tone. "Jesus came on cold straw, Jesus was warmed by the breath of an ox. 'Who is this?' the world said, 'who is this blue-cold child and this woman, plain as the winter. Is this the Word of God, this blue-cold child? Is this His will, this plain winter-woman?'

[12] Robert W. Jenson, "How the World Lost Its Story," *First Things*, October 1993, https://www.firstthings.com/article/1993/10/how-the-world-lost-its-story.

> "Listen you people!" she cried. "The world knew in its heart, the same as you know in your hearts and I know in my heart. The world said, 'Love cuts like the cold wind and the will of God is plain as the winter. Where is the summer will of God? Where are the green seasons of God's will? Where is the spring and summer of God's will?'
>
> "They had to flee into Egypt," she said in a low voice. . . . "You and I know . . . what the world hoped then. The world hoped old Herod would slay the right child, the world hoped old Herod wouldn't waste those children, but he wasted them. He didn't get the right one. Jesus grew up and raised the dead. . . ."
>
> "Jesus grew up and raised the dead," she cried, and the world shouted, 'Leave the dead lie. The dead are dead and can stay that way. What do we want with the dead alive?' Oh you people!" she shouted, "they nailed him to a cross and run a spear through His side and then they said, 'Now we can have some peace, now we can ease our minds.' And they hadn't but only said it when they wanted Him to come again. Their eyes were opened and they saw the glory they had killed." (CW, 413–14)

Only at the end does Lucette declare the ultimate either/or: Not to trust and obey the burning, purifying Word is for humanity already to be cremating itself in its own holocaust:

> "Listen world," she cried, flinging up her arms so that the cape flew out behind her, "Jesus is coming again! The mountains are going to lie down like hounds at His feet, the stars are going to perch on His shoulder and when He calls it, the sun is going to fall like a goose for His feast. Will you know the Lord Jesus then? The mountains will know him and bound forward, the stars will light on His head, the sun will drop down at His feet, but will you know the Lord Jesus then?" . . .
>
> "If you don't know Him now, you won't know Him then. Listen to me, world, listen to this warning. The Holy Word is in my mouth! . . . I've seen the Lord in a tree of fire! . . . The Word of God is a *burning* Word to burn you clean! . . . Burns the whole world, man and child, man and child the same, you people! Be saved in the Lord's fire or perish in your own!" (CW, 414–15, emphasis added)

Lest readers suspect that Flannery O'Connor is clandestinely importing a so-called Catholic theology of merit as the basis for salvation, we need look no further than N. T. Wright, the Anglican theologian who insists, together with Lucette Carmody, that we are indeed saved by our works:

> The "works" in accordance with which the Christian will be vindicated on the last day are not the unaided works of the self-help moralist. Nor are they the performance of the ethnically distinctive Jewish boundary-markers (sabbath, food-laws and circumcision). They are the things which show, rather, that one is in Christ; the things which are produced in one's life as a result of the Spirit's indwelling and operation. In this way, Romans 8.1–17 provides the real answer to Romans 2.1–16. Why is there now "no condemnation"? Because, on the one hand, God has condemned sin in the flesh of Christ; and, on the other hand, because the Spirit is at work to do, within believers, what the Law could not do—ultimately, to give life, but a life that begins in the present with the putting to death of the deeds of the body and the obedient submission to the leading of the Spirit.[13]

Surely this is the Word of the Church for our time, made audible in the preaching of Lucette Carmody. It also becomes visible in Flannery O'Connor's self-portrait.

13 N. T. Wright, "New Perspectives on Paul," July 12, 2016, https://ntwrightpage.com/2016/07/12/new-perspectives-on-paul/.

4

Flannery O'Connor's Self-Portrait in the Light of Christ Pantocrator

Flannery O'Connor had more than a passing interest in the icon of Christ Pantocrator who peers down from the central dome of Orthodox churches, signifying that he and no other is the Ruler of all things. In "Parker's Back," her last polished work before her death at age thirty-nine in 1964, she put it to memorable use. It is also one of her funniest stories. Obadiah Elihue Parker has covered his body with tattoos of sexual power and predation: "a tiger and a panther on each shoulder, a cobra coiled about a torch on his chest, hawks on his thighs" (CW, 659). Thus does he fashion himself as a tattooed conqueror of women: "He had never yet met a woman who was not attracted to them" (CW, 657). Not, that is, until he meets Bible-quoting, image-despising Sarah Ruth Cates, a fundamentalist who has utter contempt for them: "It's a heap of vanity," she snorts, "Vanity of vanities" (CW, 660). And when Parker seeks to demonstrate that he is no sort of a Christian by flinging forth a string of curses, she silences him by whacking him mercilessly with a broom.

The God whom Sarah Ruth has encased in her gnostic box is the same God whom O. E. Parker has spent his life seeking to escape. He hilariously fails to flee the Hound of Heaven when he crashes his tractor into the single and easily avoidable tree standing at the center of the field he is mowing. This calamity sets the tree ablaze and throws Parker, Moses-like, shoeless to the ground. That the God-fleeing Parker finally finds God in a cow pasture strikes the reader as funny, of course, but Parker himself is far from cheered. He hardly pauses before heading straight for a tattoo parlor. Yet the frantic Parker fails to locate the Lord among the saccharine pictures in the tattooist's catalogue: "The Good Shepherd, Forbid Them Not, The Smiling Jesus, Jesus the Physicians' Friend" (CW, 667). As he ponders them, Parker hears a voice commanding him to "GO BACK." And so he returns to the icon he cannot ignore: "the haloed head of a flat stern Byzantine Christ with all-demanding eyes" (CW, 667). Painfully but patiently Parker has his back—the only portion of his body he cannot vaingloriously behold—incised with a figure of the Lord whom he has unforgettably met. At last, Parker believes, he has found the image that will satisfy his hyper-religious wife.

Far from it. In a scene at once comic and sad, Sarah Ruth greets Parker's return with contempt for his new tattoo. When Parker demands that she behold the Pantocrator whose bearer he has now permanently become, she confesses (far more egregiously than she understands), that "It ain't anybody I know." "God don't *look* [like that]," she adds. "He's a spirit. No man shall see his face" (CW, 674). Hard-eyed Sarah Ruth drives Parker out of their house by thrashing him again with a broom, knocking him senseless and raising large welts on the face of the tattooed Christ Pantocrator. At the end Parker is seen leaning against a pecan tree, weeping. Thus is the story brought full circle to its beginning, as Christ is crucified afresh and a new believer is made to take up his cross, as it shall be until the end of time.

The Icon Tradition

In a letter to his niece Sofya Ivanovna, Dostoevsky declares that there is "only one positively beautiful figure in the world—Christ. . . . The whole of the Gospel of St. John is a statement to that effect." Yet this claim begs a further question: What *kind* of "positively beautiful figure"? Vigen Guroian points out that Dostoevsky was also drawn to a virtual anti-icon: Hans Holbein's macabre *Dead Christ in the Tomb*. Dostoevsky had seen it in an 1867 trip to Basel:

> Dostoevsky was so gripped by the painting [his wife Anna Grigoryevna reported] that he perched on a chair and stared at it for a long time, for so long, in fact, that she feared her husband would be caught and fined. *Dead Christ in the Tomb* depicts the newly deceased Christ laid out in a casket. The painting is life-size, nearly six feet long and just ten inches high. Christ's body is emaciated, blue, swollen, and riddled with the bloody wounds delivered to him. His eyes are partially open, but they show death and not life in their glassy and lusterless look. *Dead Christ in the Tomb* is everything a traditional Byzantine or Russian icon of Christ is not, for there is not

> a hint of the Resurrection in it. And from all the evidence, this gruesome contrast shook Dostoevsky's religious imagination.[1]

Natalie Carnes clarifies the cause of Dostoevsky's shattering encounter:

> Beauty is rarely found far from ugliness. . . . It is not that finding beauty apart from ugliness is impossible . . . but that the greater and the more profound the beauty, the greater the ugliness in which it is implicated, for the profoundest beauties participate in the eschatological Beauty, which is to say, the One who is Beauty Crucified.[2]

Albert Raboteau, a Princeton professor of religion, underwent a radical re-conversion after viewing an icon exhibition at his university. These images prompted Raboteau thus to identify the basic tonality of Christian existence as "a sorrowful joy."

Icons seek to convey the paradoxical and often conflicted beauty of God in Jesus Christ and his saints. What the Gospel proclaims to us by words, declared the Council of Constantinople (869–870), the icon proclaims and renders present for us by color. Icons are built, therefore, on a theology of spiritual presence rather than natural representation. They are not images that *we behold* in order to discern an earthly rendering of the Holy. Rather do they *behold us*, as God's own splendor radiates through them, filling those who rightly venerate them with life-transforming Reality.

The Face as Self-Revealing Mask

The Greek word translated as "person" is *prosopon*. It refers to the face or else to a mask as a depiction of the face. The face is not a superficial thing: Its significance does not lie on its superficies, its surface. Since the soul is the form of the body, as Aquinas taught, the face is literally an expression—a pressing outward—of inward reality. Except in the most skilled hands, cameras are virtually useless in revealing our faces, so limited is their capacity to probe depths. Flannery O'Connor complained to Elizabeth Hester about this travesty: "Your face ought to be sacred to you but it sure is not. I am always glad when some judge stands out and won't

1 Quoted in Vigen Guroian, "Can Beauty Save the World?" *Touchstone*, November/December 2017.

2 Also quoted in Guroian, "Can Beauty Save the World?"

let photographers into his courtroom. Photographers are the lowest breed of men" (HB, 534).

To project their voices in order to be heard in amphitheaters that seated thousands, actors on the Greek stage wore huge masks. These masks also offered a rough idea of the actor's character. Thus are face and mask and character deeply linked. Our *prosopon* indicates who we are, our deepest identity, our very being. *Aprosopon*, by contrast, is the Greek word sometimes used to name slaves, those who in the worst sense have no face. Malefactors who appear in icons (for example, members of the Golgotha mob) are always shown in profile: They have no full, no true face.

"The face," declares Fr. Stephen Freeman, "is not only our primary presentation to the world, and our primary means of relationship, it is also, somehow, that which is most definitively identified with our existence as persons." "I cannot see the face of another without looking at them," Freeman adds. "To see your face, I must reveal my face. That face-to-face encounter is pretty much the deepest and oldest experience we have as human beings (first experienced with our mother in nursing). For the whole of our lives, our faces are the primary points of experience and reaction. We cannot truly know the other without encountering them face-to-face." Revelation 6:16, Freeman concludes, "does not simply speak of the wrath of the Lamb, nor merely of His presence. It is specifically a fear of His face. Our experience of the face is an experience of nakedness and vulnerability. On the positive side, the result is identification, communion and oneness. On the negative side, it is the pain of shame and the felt need to hide. I can think of nothing else in nature that so closely parallels and reveals the fundamental character of our relationship with God."[3]

The philosopher Emanuel Levinas is a penetrating analyst of the significance of human faces. He argues that their uniqueness entails not only their irreplaceability but also our own responsibility to them. It is a responsibility, Levinas maintains, that "cannot be refused, [it is] of an order alien to knowledge; as if, for all eternity, the I were the first one called to this responsibility; [it is] non-transferable and thus unique, thus I, the chosen hostage, the chosen one." It also entails an ethics of ultimate sociality:

> For all eternity, one man is answerable for an other. From unique to unique. Whether he looks at me or not, he "regards me"; I must

3 Fr. Stephen Freeman, "To See Him Face to Face," *Glory to God for All Things*, March 24, 2023, https://blogs.ancientfaith.com/glory2godforallthings/2023/03/24/to-see-him-face-to-face/.

> answer for him. I call face that which thus in another concerns the I—concerns me—reminding me, from behind the countenance he puts on in his portrait, of his abandonment, his defenselessness and his mortality, and his appeal to my ancient responsibility, as if he were unique in the world—beloved.

More drastically still, the life—and thus the death—of these other faces is likely to matter more to me than my own death:

> An appeal of the face of my fellowman, which, in its ethical urgency, postpones or cancels the obligations [that] the "summoned I" has toward itself and in which the concern for the death of the other can be more important to the I than its concern as an I for itself. The authenticity of the I, in my view, is this listening [to] the first one called, this attention to the other without subrogation, and thus already faithfulness to values despite one's own mortality.[4]

Flannery O'Connor's celebrated self-portrait is imbued with Levinas' concern for the uniqueness and irreplaceability of the human face—not least of all her own. Far from indulging any sort of vainglory, O'Connor deflects attention away from mere subjective considerations by modeling her image on the unique and irreplaceable Face found in the sixth-century icon of Christ Pantocrator from St. Catherine's monastery on Mt. Sinai. More remarkable still, she includes a sly suggestion about her own responsibility to it.

Flannery O'Connor's Self-Portrait and the Mt. Sinai Christ Pantocrator

Pantocrator, by most common reckonings, is a compound formed from *pas*, the Greek word for "all," and the verb *krateo*, "to have power, to rule." The word Pantocrator in both the Septuagint and the Book of Revelation is commonly translated as "Almighty," the Hebrew for "Lord of Hosts," or else rendered as Kyrios Pantocrator, the Lord Almighty. The most famous icon of Christ Pantocrator is the sixth-century version found at St. Catherine's Monastery on Mt. Sinai.

It cannot be denied the Mt. Sinai Pantocrator is based on Roman imperial portraits. Yet this is no domineering Emperor; this is the rightly ruling

4 Emmanuel Levinas, "The Other, Utopia, and Justice," in *Entre Nous: On Thinking-of-the-Other* (New York: Columbia University Press, 1998), 227.

Christ. The fingers of his right hand offer blessing in the Byzantine fashion: The first two fingers are joined and raised to recall both his human and divine natures, while the other two fingers are united with the thumb in the sign of the Trinity. In his left hand he grasps a thick papyrus codex, probably the Gospel of John, the evangel that most boldly announces the Incarnation: "And the Word became flesh and dwelt among us . . . full of grace and truth" (1:14). The eyes of this most ancient Christ Pantocrator are noticeably asymmetrical. His right eye grips the beholder with commanding clarity, looking straight ahead, glowing with mercy. His other eye is cast slightly leftward, darkened with the judgment that must accompany true mercy, as the slightly arched brow may suggest. The Pantocrator's head is not crowned with a halo of holiness; it is surrounded, instead, by a nimbus bursting with radiant light.

I contend that Flannery O'Connor patterned her self-portrait after the Christ Pantocrator of Mt. Sinai. This is not for a moment to suggest that

Christ Pantocrator, 6th century (encaustic on panel)
Photo © Zev Radovan / Bridgeman Images

Flannery O'Connor, self-portrait, courtesy of the Mary
Flannery O'Connor Charitable Trust

she mounted a copy beside her as she painted. She declared in a letter to Janet McKane from 1963 that she had drawn her self-image ten years earlier "after a very acute seige [sic] of lupus. I was taking cortisone which gives you what they call a moon face and my hair had fallen out to a large extent from the high fever, so I looked pretty much like the portrait. When I painted it I didn't look either at myself or at the bird. I knew what we both looked like" (CW, 1187).

O'Connor makes no mention of Christ Pantocrator, but the resemblances become patent when they are set alongside each other. Like his, her eyes are willfully askew. Her right eyebrow is slightly raised. Her ears can hardly be seen. Her lips are almost balefully unsmiling. And her yellow straw hat virtually replicates his golden nimbus. Yet here the resemblances end for, in place of the Gospel, she is cradling—not one of her beloved peafowl, but a pheasant cock, the fiercest of its kind. Its black eyes seem ready to spot potential prey, its yellow beak ready to dig into their flesh. "I like very much the look of the pheasant cock," O'Connor wrote. "He has horns and a face like the Devil" (CW, 1187).

It should be evident that Flannery O'Connor is not depicting herself as being in *league* with this demonic figure. I maintain that the twenty-eight-year-old self-portraitist embraces the demonic pheasant cock as a sign of her peculiar evangelical vocation—her Levinas-like responsibility to the one irreplaceable Face. She is subtly confessing, I believe, that she puts the demonic in her own employ so as to deceive the Deceiver—and thus to undeceive her characters about his operations. There can be no encounter with incarnate Goodness without also wrestling with discarnate Evil, "our ancient foe" who seeks "to work us woe," as Martin Luther names him in "A Mighty Fortress." "Christ fights with the devil in a curious way," Luther adds, "—the devil with great numbers, cleverness, and steadfastness, and Christ with few people, with weakness, simplicity, and contempt—and yet Christ wins." "There are two equal and opposite errors into which our race can fall about the devils," C. S. Lewis notes in his preface to the original 1941 edition of *The Screwtape Letters*. "One is to disbelieve in their existence. The other is to believe, and to feel an excessive and unhealthy interest in them. They themselves [the devils] are equally pleased by both errors."[5] As we shall see, Flannery O'Connor's fiction avoids both of these demonic deceptions.

Naming the Devil

St. Matthew's gospel uses three terms for the Prince of Darkness: Tempter, Satan, and Devil. Jesus addresses Satan by his proper name when the chief apostle urges him to avoid Jerusalem, lest he be hanged there. In perhaps the Lord's harshest condemnation, he commands Peter to "Get thee behind me, Satan: thou art a stumbling-block unto me: for thou mindest not the things of God, but the things of men" (Matt 16:23, KJV). "The Greek word *diabolos* (*devil*) means a *false accuser* or *slanderer*," Fr. Paul Scalia explains. "It comes from *dia-ballein*, which means *to throw apart*. After all, a slanderer is someone who confuses things, *throws* them into confusion, and leads to false accusations. A *diabolos* is someone who brings disorder and division—which is an accurate description of the

5 C. S. Lewis, *The Screwtape Letters and Screwtape Proposes a Toast*, annotated ed. (New York: Harper One, 2013), xlvii.

Devil's work. In fact, it's a fair summary not just of all that he does but all that he *can* do."[6]

The subtlest of the Serpent's wiles, O'Connor said, is to convince us that he does not exist. She is determined to force him out of his guises, indeed to deface him. "To insure our sense of mystery," she wrote, "we need a sense of evil which sees the devil as a real spirit who must be made to name himself, and not simply to name himself as vague evil, but to name himself with his specific personality for every occasion." (MM, 117). "The Devil is most tortured to have to call his own name. I want to be certain," she added, "that the Devil gets identified as the Devil and not simply taken for this or that psychological tendency" (HB, 360).

By this O'Connor did not mean that Satan himself appears in her fiction, declaring (with Milton's Satan) "Evil, be thou my good." Exactly to the contrary: "the devil plays the greatest role in the production of that fiction from which he himself is absent as an actor" (MM, 189). Thus does she make him evident by indirection; i.e., by his seductive power over her characters. Hence her attraction to the warning found in 1 Peter 5:8 (KJV): "Be sober, be vigilant; because your adversary the devil, as a roaring lion, walketh about, seeking whom he may devour." She also had repeated recourse to St. Cyril of Jerusalem's instruction for catechumens: "The dragon sits by the side of the road, watching those who pass. Beware lest he devour you. We go to the Father of Souls, but it is necessary to pass by the dragon" (MM, 35).

It must be stressed that Flannery O'Connor embraced no privatized notions of the demonic. Luciferian deceptions are social and cultural before they are personal and individual. The latter are manifestations of the former. "Our salvation is a drama played out with the devil, a devil who is not simply generalized evil," she wrote, "but an evil intelligence determined on [his] own supremacy" (MM, 168). He seeks nothing less than cosmic domination. Thus did she honor the stark biblical claim that Satan is the ruler of this realm (cf. John 14:30). "I have found," she confessed, "that my subject in fiction is the action of grace in territory largely held by the devil" (MM, 118).

In Eastern and Western traditions alike, evil is understood to have no proper existence of its own. It is *privatio boni*, the absence, the twisting, the perversion of the Good. Yet precisely because it is Nothing—a

6 Fr. Paul D. Scalia, "Three Faces of Evil," *The Catholic Thing*, February 26, 2023, https://www.thecatholicthing.org/2023/02/26/three-faces-of-evil/.

no-thing—it can assume innumerable forms of some-thing. The devil's chief guise, according to Flannery O'Connor, is nihilism. "If you live today," we have heard her declare, "you breathe in nihilism. In or out of the Church, it's the gas you breathe. If I hadn't had the Church to fight it with or to tell me the necessity of fighting it," she wittily confessed, "I would be the stinkingest logical positivist you ever saw" (HB, 97).[7] Nihilism, for O'Connor, entails the claim that life has no transcendent meaning, no objective purpose, no ultimate origin or aim—nothing but the subjective "values" we impose on it, so that the strong may dominate the weak. In her terms, it is all a matter of demonic power.

Destroying the Idea of God in Man

Were she living at this hour, where might Flannery O'Connor locate the deadliest deceptions of the Prince of Darkness? They are to be found, I believe, in the steadily increased instrumentalizing of human life. When human beings are reduced to objects for manipulation akin to figures on a chessboard, they can be made to serve whatever purposes their masters desire, no matter how pernicious. Ever less are they regarded as having intrinsic, irreplaceable, sacred worth. O'Connor marked this steady shrinkage of human value upon learning that a technique had been devised for breeding the wings off chickens, so as to create an abundance of tender white meat. She likened this "breakthrough" to the breeding "out of the moral sense of certain sections of the population." "This is a generation of wingless chickens," she concluded, "which I suppose is what Nietzsche meant when he said that God was dead" (HB, 90).

O'Connor was too theologically keen to entertain the absurd notion that we puny humans could destroy the Maker and Redeemer of the cosmos. Yet she agreed with Dostoevsky that it is quite possible to destroy the image of God in man. Ironically, it is the Devil himself who voices this horror to the hallucinating Ivan near the end of *The Brothers Karamazov*:

> I maintain that nothing need be destroyed, that we only need to destroy *the idea of God in man*, that's how we have to set to work. It's that, that we must begin with. Oh, blind race of men who have no

[7] Logical positivism is a philosophical movement that arose in Vienna in the 1920s. It held that scientific knowledge alone is factual and thus that all metaphysical doctrines must be rejected as meaningless. For O'Connor, it is precisely those doctrines that prevented her from murdering her mind.

> understanding! As soon as men have all of them denied God—and I believe that period, analogous with geological periods, will come to pass—the old conception of the universe will fall of itself without cannibalism, and, what's more the old morality, and then everything will begin anew. Men will unite to take from life all it can give, but only for joy and happiness in the present world. Man will be lifted up with a spirit of divine Titanic pride and the man-god will appear. From hour to hour extending his conquest of nature infinitely by his will and his science, man will feel such lofty joy from hour to hour in doing it that it will make up for all his old dreams of the joys of heaven. Everyone will know that he is mortal and will accept death proudly and serenely like a God. His pride will teach him that it's useless for him to repine at life's being a moment, and he will love his brother without need of reward. Love will be sufficient only for a moment of life, but the very consciousness of its momentariness will intensify its fire, which now is dissipated in dreams of 'eternal love beyond the grave' . . . and so on and so on in the same style. Charming![8]

We are now witnessing, I believe, a Luciferian attempt "to destroy the idea of God in man": to reinvent human nature itself, to create a new species. We no longer understand man as *homo viator*—man as pilgrim on the journey to God—but as *homo homini lupus*—man as the wolf who devours man. The human body remains an inviolable sacred gift, not the site for demonic mutilations. It is nothing less than the "temple of the Holy Ghost," as O'Connor demonstrates in a remarkable story.

The Holy Hermaphrodite in "A Temple of the Holy Ghost"

If previous ages may have felt less than ours, O'Connor repeatedly iterated, they saw more. "In the novelist's case," she wrote, "prophecy is a matter of seeing near things with their extensions of meaning and thus of seeing far things close up. The novelist is a realist of distances" (MM, 44). With such prophetic foresight of seeing far things close up, Flannery O'Connor made this remarkable claim in 1955. It may become the basis for her eventually being declared a doctor (magisterial teacher) of the Church:

8 Fyodor Dostoevsky, *The Brothers Karamazov*, Norton Critical Edition, trans. Constance Garnett, rev. Ralph Matlaw (New York: Norton, 1976), 615–16 (emphasis added).

> I am always astonished at the emphasis the Church puts on the body. It is not the soul she says will rise but the body, glorified. I have always thought that purity was the most mysterious of the virtues, but it occurs to me that it would never have entered the human consciousness to conceive of purity if we were not to look forward to a resurrection of the body, which will be flesh and spirit united in peace, in the way they were in Christ. The resurrection of Christ seems the high point in the law of nature. (CW, 953)

These are not high-soaring theological abstractions. O'Connor earthed them in a stunning story, "A Temple of the Holy Ghost."

It is the story of a brilliant preadolescent girl who delights in ridiculing the stupidities she discerns in everyone but herself. Yet this nameless young smartalice is no monster of presumption. She even dreams of becoming a martyr, "if they killed her quick" (CW, 204). She has no use for suffering. But neither will she tolerate the mockery of her hormone-driven teenaged cousins when they make howling fun of Sister Perpetua. She is the naïve nun who had taught the girls how to fend off the advances of groping boys. They were to employ a formula taken from 1 Corinthians 6: "Stop sir! I am a Temple of the Holy Ghost." Against the sexy cousins' wild hilarity at such a claim, the girl-child finds nothing ridiculous about it. She is gratefully astonished, instead, to hear that she is nothing less than the dwelling place of God. "It made her feel as if somebody had given her a present" (CW, 199).

She learns what it means to be the bodily locus of God's own Spirit when the sex-obsessed cousins report on a strange sight they had seen at the county fair: a grotesque freak, an hermaphrodite. He is double-sexed. According to the norms of our age, he is disabled in the worst way, robbed of all sexual satisfaction via a hideous blunder of nature. In our time, he would surely be sent away for sexual reassignment surgery. Against all readerly expectation, however, O'Connor has the story's nameless heroine offer a drastic alternative. She enters a dreamlike state of prophetic vision, imagining the hermaphrodite graciously embracing rather than bitterly bemoaning his bodily deformity. She turns him into a country preacher leading his people in a litany of praise and acceptance:

> "God done this to me and I praise him."
> "Amen. Amen."
> "He could strike you thisaway."
> "Amen. Amen."

"But he has not."
"Amen."
"Raise yourself up. A temple of the Holy Ghost. You! You are God's temple, don't you know? Don't you know? God's Spirit has a dwelling in you, don't you know?"
"Amen. Amen." (CW, 207)

Conclusion

"More than in the Devil," Flannery O'Connor confessed, "I am interested in the indication of Grace, the moment when you know that Grace has been offered and accepted" (HB, 367). Such divine self-offering and such divinely enabled acceptance are the true means for keeping our species from demonically refashioning itself into something irrecoverably evil. She was not arrogant but modest, I maintain, in patterning her self-portrait after the Mt. Sinai Pantocrator. She models her own image after his, not that we might have faces like hers, but like his—finally sanctified, made fully whole, body and soul knit together in complex and seamless unity.

Nowhere more convincingly than in *The Violent Bear It Away* does O'Connor deal with the terrors that ensue when this divine image is threatened with demonic destruction, and nowhere more persuasively does she treat its baptismal redemption. Hence our turn to it.

5

Baptizing and Prophesying

The Fierce Struggle of Good and Evil in The Violent Bear It Away

The title of Flannery O'Connor's *The Violent Bear It Away* contains both a conundrum and the key for unlocking it. The novel's name is taken from the Douay-Rheims translation of Matthew 11:12: "And from the days of John the Baptist until now, the kingdom of heaven *suffereth violence*, and the violent bear it away" (emphasis original). Many biblical scholars interpret this passage as a reference to those who would heretically seize the Kingdom by force, brutally turning it into a means of destruction rather than redemption. The phrase may also refer to Zealots who wanted to rout the Romans, or else to priests who bullied their way into control of the synagogues or, even more particularly, to arrogant leaders of the Jewish temple with its wealth, prestige, and political power. In every case, the scholarly consensus holds that the biblical reference to seizing the Kingdom has entirely negative import.

Yet there are other ways of reading Matthew's strange saying about the violence that besets the Reign of God. Flannery O'Connor praised medieval exegetes for discerning not merely one but at least three other means of interpreting biblical texts. Beyond the *literal* reading of Scripture (in this case, seeking the historical meaning such as the one cited above), there is also the *allegorical* (linking a person or event with an analogous one; e.g., Moses' deliverance of Israel from Egyptian bondage with Jesus' redemption of humanity from slavery to sin), the *tropological* (gleaning moral implications for the Christian life, to do good and abjure evil), as well as the *anagogical* (discerning the spiritual and eschatological significance of the text, especially life in the world to come). Such theologically rich readings of Scripture ensure its living, full-bodied appropriation by and for the Church.

Hence this gloss on Matthew 11:12 given in the 1899 Challoner version of the Douay-Rheims Bible that O'Connor kept close at hand: "[The Kingdom] is not to be obtained but by main force, by using violence upon ourselves, by mortification and penance, and resisting our perverse inclinations."[1] The violence that makes raids on the Rule of God is thus regarded not as satanic but salutary, even necessary. Christians seize the Kingdom not by wielding the Gospel as an axe to slay the world's evils but by practicing spiritual violence against their own sinfulness. In *The Violent Bear It Away*, O'Connor's most complex and provocative work, such violence consists in either seizing or else spurning the call to the baptismal and prophetic life as it is figured in Mason and Francis Marion Tarwater.

My purpose here is to demonstrate that both interpretations of the assaults on the Kingdom of God—both the satanic and the holy—are at work in *The Violent Bear It Away*. Yet they cannot be seen aright until we have first attended to three related matters: (1) the waning American regard for the demonic; (2) the proper Christian understanding of evil as Nothingness; and (3) the anti-Christian estimate of the satanic as symbolic at best, energetic at worst.

The Place of Satan in American Culture

In *The Death of Satan*, Andrew Delbanco traces our waning American regard for the demonic, as our churches and our culture have come to accord the Devil ever lessening importance. Already in the Puritans, Delbanco discerns a profound ambiguity about the Evil One. On one hand, their radical consciousness of sin made them ascribe acute reality to satanic power, as in the Salem Witch Trials. Yet, on the other hand, Lucifer ceased to be the macabre monstrosity of both ancient and medieval Christian tradition. The Puritans worried that such personifications may miss the ubiquity and subtlety of demonic temptation, finding in them a convenient means for transferring their own culpability for sin to the Prince of Darkness.

Jonathan Edwards, for example, was concerned almost entirely with human freedom and responsibility for resisting evil, permitting no one to blame either social circumstances or demonic forces for their own faults. Much against the intentions of the Puritans, however, the Devil was rapidly reduced to a subjective construction of the imagination not to be credited by our most eminent writers. It is obvious that such Transcendentalists

[1] Douay-Rheims Bible, http://www.drbo.org/chapter/47011.htm.

as Emerson and Thoreau, with their belief in latent human perfectibility, would slight Satan. Yet neither could Hawthorne or Melville, despite their riveted attention to human maleficence, envision Satan as its real source. So fully has he absconded from American mentality in our time that the psychologist Henry Murray has declared him finally dead—a mere figment, "no more than a vestigial image, a broken-spirited relic of a perished past, a ludicrous ham actor with no greater part to play in man's imagination than the vermiform appendix in his gut."[2]

It seems at first surprising that such an astute reader of American literature as Delbanco would make no mention of Flannery O'Connor, since the Devil figures so prominently in her fiction. Yet Delbanco gradually reveals the reason for his silence: He may fear that her attribution of evil to a satanic "other" leaves our own cruel perfidy and malignant complicity unimpeached. The horrors of the deadliest of all modern centuries, for him as a secular Jew, are the work of invisible but still explicable forces—namely, human irresponsibility and wrongdoing in all of their manifold expressions of self-hatred and self-deception. Delbanco thus finds the most adequate explanation of evil in such Protestant theologians as Reinhold Niebuhr and Paul Tillich. For Tillich, the demonic "is the elevation of something conditional to unconditional significance," and thus an entirely human phenomenon. Niebuhr is but slightly more willing than Tillich to concede that evil is a "principle or force . . . antecedent to any evil human action."[3]

In perhaps his most celebrated paradox, Niebuhr claims that, while the Fall is inevitable, it is not necessary. Always and everywhere, human beings have sinned and will continue to sin, even as they remain responsible for their willing embrace of their Adamic proclivity. Evil precedes and antedates all human doing of it. Yet Niebuhr turns this into an anthropological more than a theological claim, since the Devil is nowhere featured in his work. Delbanco's own conclusion remains thoroughly Tillichian and Niebuhrian: Satan is "a symbol of our own deficient love, our potential for envy and rancor toward creation." Evil abides as nothing other than a permanent privation that "offers something that the Devil himself could never have intended: the miraculous paradox of demanding the best of ourselves."[4]

2 Quoted in Andrew Delbanco, *The Death of Satan: How Americans Have Lost the Sense of Evil* (New York: Farrar, Straus & Giroux, 1995), 4.

3 Delbanco, *Death of Satan*, 189, 46.

4 Delbanco, *Death of Satan*, 234–35.

Evil as a Privation of the Good, an Absence of True Being

Even if little credence can be given to such a self-generated "demand" that leaves our "best selves" undefined, Delbanco offers a small opening to a larger comprehension of evil with his use of the word "privation." As we have seen, St. Augustine construes evil as *privatio boni*, the absence of true being, the perversion or deformation of the Good. Augustine's revolutionary insight—derived originally from the Neoplatonists, repeated by Boethius, and maintained throughout Christian tradition—insists on the insubstantiality of evil. Evil has no life of its own, since it is the willful distortion of the Good, the prideful misshaping of the divinely ordered creation.[5]

As Delbanco notes, the image of the knot enables Augustine "to speak of the complexity and intransigence of evil without granting it any essence of its own. A distortion of something whose essence precedes its disfigurement, evil is in the twistedness, not in the rope."[6] Hence the Christian rejection of the Manichean error of making evil the co-equal counterpart of the good, indeed its virtual provocateur, arousing it to necessary warfare against evil.

This is not to say that there are no biblical grounds for such warfare: "Finally, be strong in the Lord and in the strength of his might. Put on the whole armor of God, that you may be able to stand against the wiles of the Devil. For we are not contending against flesh and blood, but against the principalities, against the powers, against the world rulers of this present darkness, against the spiritual hosts of wickedness in the heavenly places" (Eph 6:10–13, ESV). Satan's most cunning deceit, it follows, is the delusion that we ourselves can defeat evil. Karl Barth thunders against this delusion:

[5] This understanding of evil has its counterpart in the doctrine of *creatio ex nihilo*—the conviction that God generates the universe out of no previously existing matter; for if he did so, then something would have existed alongside him, making him less than the original and ultimate Reality. Literally understood, Genesis 1 seems to contradict *creatio ex nihilo*, for it speaks of the earth as being aboriginally "without form and void," so that "the Spirit of God was moving over the waters." Yet the Hebrew term for "waters" is *tohu-wabohu*, or desert-ocean; i.e., a self-contradictory nothing. Thus did Augustine employ *privatio boni* as the most adequate means of dealing with the many biblical personifications of evil without regarding them as representations of some primordial Manichean force set over against God as his deadly equal and dualistic rival.

[6] Delbanco, *Death of Satan*, 49.

> If "I" can cope with [nothingness], opposing "myself" to it victorious in defeat; if I can acknowledge and resist it by defying it, it is not true nothingness. It may well be significant, violent, threatening and extremely aggressive, but if I can confront it with sovereign power, if I can deal with it, if I can even play with it in changing situations, if I can set it behind me, I cannot convince myself that I have to do with the true and deadly dangerous adversary of myself and man and life.[7]

The paradoxical Christian counterclaim is that, while evil has horrific power and devastating effect, it is ultimately to be regarded as emptiness and nothingness. It is something alien rather than essential to God's good creation. It has no power to create, only to damage and destroy. It exists but parasitically, leeching off the good, as the very name of C. S. Lewis' demonic Screwtape makes evident: He is a tapeworm battening off his host. The negative and entirely derivative character of evil means that Christians refuse to attribute divinity to the Devil. All Christian creeds profess *Credo in Deus*, none affirms *Credo in diabolus*. Hence Lewis' thoroughly biblical and anti-dualistic claim that Satan's adversarial opposite is not God but the archangel Michael.[8]

Exactly because Satan has no substance or essence, he can feign manifold appearances, the less obvious the more deadly. Indeed, he *must* assume these many masks, since he always acts in the semblance of some alleged good, having no positive identity of his own. Not by happenstance is he regarded as the supreme illusionist, the "subtlest beast of the field," "the Father of Lies." Therein lies the perverse power of the Evil One as well as the key to interpreting the guises he assumes in Scripture. He appears as a snake in Genesis, as Lucifer in Isaiah, as Beelzebub in Luke, as Belial in 2 Corinthians, and as Satan himself in many other places—not only as he tempts Jesus in the wilderness, but also as he is finally defeated in the Apocalypse: "The great dragon . . . that ancient serpent, who is called the Devil and Satan, the deceiver of the whole world—he was thrown down to the earth, and his angels were thrown down with him" (Rev 12:9).

St. Augustine echoes St. Paul's fundamental claim about our fallen species: "they exchanged the truth about God for a lie and worshiped and

7 Karl Barth, *Church Dogmatics*, vol. 3, pt. 3, *The Doctrine of Creation*, trans. G. W. Bromiley and T. F. Torrance (New York: T&T Clark, 2009), 346.

8 C. S. Lewis, *The Screwtape Letters*, rev. ed. (New York: Macmillan, 1961), vii.

served the creature rather than the Creator" (Rom 1:25). Yet neither the chief apostle nor the bishop of Hippo presumes to explain *why* God's wholly good creatures, whether angelic or human, would pervert his wholly good creation without cause. Strictly speaking, therefore, evil is unaccountable; it is an absurd descent into the Void. The wrongful pursuit of inferior things is a pursuit of nothing. This is not to deny that evil originates in either heavenly or earthly beings, nor to gainsay their responsibility for it, nor to dismiss its mysterious place within God's ultimate design. Rather is it to agree with John Milbank that evil must be denied all rational explanation. It must be refused the light and speech that it abhors, as he crustily declares:

> According to Augustine, the origin of evil must be passed over as "darkness and silence." . . . Because evil is uncaused, there is indeed a sense in which it possesses us like an anti-cause proceeding from a Satanic black hole: as J.-L. Marion argues—the non-existence of the Devil is the existence of the Devil. But when evil possesses us, not only are we responsible for this possession, it is also the case that this possession delivers the very phenomenon of autonomous responsibility. Evil is just that for which . . . we are solely responsible. Evil is self-governing autonomy—evil is the Kantian good, the modern good.[9]

There Can Be No Rivalry between God and Humanity

The Anglican theologian Rowan Williams makes clear why there can be no rivalry between God and humanity. The incarnate Christ delivers us, the former Archbishop of Canterbury declares, from such a dichotomy,

> . . . from a theology in which God is in danger of being seen simply as a very important or uniquely powerful agent in the universe competing with other agents in the universe for space or control. That God is in no imaginable sense the rival of humanity, that the relation between finite and infinite agency can never be one in which more of one means less of the other, and (crucially) that God can have no 'interests' to defend over against the interest of the creatures God has made out of unconstrained and selfless love—all this is part of what makes the classical Christological synthesis [that Christ is fully human and fully divine] still a spiritually and morally serious

9 John Milbank, *Being Reconciled: Ontology and Pardon* (London: Routledge, 2003), 18.

proposal for understanding what is to be the object of creative and limitless generosity; or, in simple terms, for hearing the gospel.

Because God has no need to create worldly space for his action, and since he does not compete with any particular activity inside the universe, atheism in the strict sense is impossible. God cannot be done away with. There are only two possibilities for human existence: either the idea of God in man can be killed and human life rendered monstrous, or else man can embrace his life in God and thus be made utterly alive.[10]

Baptismal Exorcism

It is likely that Flannery O'Connor developed her particular regard for the satanic from the Church's baptismal liturgy, with its exorcism of the Devil and all his pomps. In the early centuries, catechumens were baptized on Easter while stretching out their hands in the fashion of a military *sacramentum*, the public swearing of an oath. In a crucially symbolic act, they faced westward as they renounced the *pompa diaboli*.[11] St. Cyril of Jerusalem describes the significance of baptismal exorcism in analogies that John Milbank would employ sixteen centuries later: "As the West is the region of visible darkness, and since Satan, who has darkness for his portion, has his empire in darkness, so, when you turn symbolically toward the West, you renounce this dark and obscure tyrant." The baptismal liturgy of the ancient Church came to its climax as the catechumens were literally re-oriented, as Jean Daniélou explains: "The profession of faith made while facing the East completed the abjuration made while facing the West."[12]

O'Connor herself used a baptismal warning from St. Cyril as the epigraph for *A Good Man Is Hard to Find*, her first collection of stories: "THE DRAGON IS BY THE SIDE OF THE ROAD, WATCHING THOSE WHO PASS. BEWARE LEST HE DEVOUR YOU. WE GO TO THE FATHER OF SOULS, BUT IT IS NECESSARY TO PASS BY THE DRAGON."[13] The

10 Rowan Williams, *Christ the Heart of Creation* (New York: Bloomsbury Continuum, 2018), 11.

11 Jean Daniélou, *The Bible and the Liturgy* (Notre Dame, Ind.: University of Notre Dame, 1956), 21.

12 Daniélou, *Bible and the Liturgy*, 30.

13 Cyril continues his admonition against the Devil as follows: "How can you avoid him? Have your feet shod with the gospel of peace, so that, if he bites you, it

great serpent must be renounced in order to break the pact that the whole of humankind implicitly made with Satan in Adam's subjection of his will to demonic supremacy, as we have heard O'Connor herself declare:

> To insure our sense of mystery, we need a sense of evil which sees the devil as a real spirit who must be made to name himself, and not simply to name himself as vague evil, but to name himself with his specific personality for every occasion. Literature, like virtue, does not thrive in an atmosphere where the devil is not recognized as existing both in himself and as a dramatic necessity for the writer. (MM, 117)

Baptism is closely linked to demonic temptation because it entails a transfer of allegiance from Satan to Christ, drawing on the power of Jesus' own wilderness foreswearing of fealty to the Evil One. "We must hasten to go before the judge," declared Theodore of Mopsuestia in the fifth century, "to establish our claims to show that by rights we did not belong to Satan from the beginning, but to God Who made us in His Own Image."[14] Thus does it become evident that, for Flannery O'Connor as for the most venerable Christian understanding, Satan is something far more sinister than the sum total of human ill will: He is a ravaging presence who stalks his prey as an exceedingly clever deceiver—except as he is driven out, whether sooner or later, by baptismal undeception.

Against Freud and Jung on Evil as Symbolic and Energetic

The fiction of Flannery O'Connor, especially *The Violent Bear It Away*, resists the relegation of Satan to an abstract principle and thus to his ultimate irrelevance. She envisions Luciferian evil in traditional terms as a personal power determined to achieve his own supremacy. When Satan appears in her fiction, she candidly observed, he is not to be understood as "this or that psychological tendency" (HB, 360). She cites Baudelaire's celebrated dictum that the Devil's greatest wile is to convince us he does not exist, and she declares his considerable success in our time. Yet for all that is traditional in her conception of Satan, she is concerned not to make him obvious, lest he be easily dismissed as a bogeyman.

---

will do you no evil. If you see any evil thought coming into your spirit, know that it is the serpent of the sea who is setting snares for you. Guard your soul so that he cannot seize it" (quoted in Daniélou, *Bible and the Liturgy*, 24).

14 Quoted in Daniélou, *Bible and the Liturgy*, 21.

Instead, her demons disguise themselves in thoroughly Freudian and Jungian terms. Freud regarded Satan as nothing other than a symbol, albeit a powerful one, of repressed erotic desires or else of neuroses lying deep within the unconscious, often negatively projected "onto individuals or groups that we identify as enemies or potential enemies."[15] In the work of Jung, Freud's student, Lucifer represents the massive destructive energy resident in the universe as it stands over against the equally enormous constructive powers that Jung links to the divine. Yet for Jung, Lucifer's name still applies: He is the light-bearer whose demonic negativity dwells in a mandala-like complementarity with divine positivity. Only as good incorporates evil into itself, Jung teaches, can higher wisdom and wholeness be attained.[16]

It is noteworthy that, when I have asked students to identify the voice that speaks inwardly to young Francis Marion Tarwater from the very beginning of the novel, they have responded in Jungian and Freudian ways. They have almost always answered that this "stranger" who gradually becomes Tarwater's "friend" is the boy's subconscious mind, his inward self, his alter ego. Such obtuseness is as predictable as it is inexcusable. Yet it plays perfectly into O'Connor's fictional purposes. Far from being an artistic mistake, her ploy enables her readers, at least potentially, to experience young Francis Marion's terrible awakening to the true identity of his inner voice.

Old Mason, Young Tarwater, and the Life of Prophecy

Francis Marion Tarwater is the great-nephew of Mason Tarwater, an eighty-four-year-old backwoods prophet who has commissioned the fourteen-year-old youth to become his successor in the life of prophecy. The boy's first task of filial loyalty is to provide a reverent burial for old Mason when he dies. The elderly Elijah instructs his would-be Elisha to bury him deep enough to prevent the dogs from digging him up, as well as to plant the sign of the Savior at the head of his grave. Francis' second summons is to baptize his cousin Bishop, the mentally-deprived child of his uncle George Rayber. Rayber is an atheist psychologist who believes that, like all other religious practices, baptism is a vain and useless rite, especially when conferred upon a virtually mindless four-year old. Yet

15 Jeffrey Burton Russell, *The Devil: Perceptions of Evil from Antiquity to Early Christianity* (Ithaca, N.Y.: Cornell University Press, 1987), 229.

16 Russell, *The Devil*, 229, 233–34.

according to old Mason, young Francis' obedience to these commands will set the boy on his way to becoming a full-fledged prophet.

In his violent seizure of the Kingdom, this uncouth *vates* is an exemplary teacher of the fundamentals of the Faith. Mason Tarwater does not accept the late-modern attempt to turn children into autonomous adults who will make up their own private minds, deciding and defining things for themselves. Such training is not meant to form moral character but to produce conventional consumers, choosers of one's own "lifestyle" from a smorgasbord of options wherein religious faith becomes merely another "preference." Instead, Mason Tarwater calls his grand-nephew to live according to the commitments that are intrinsic to baptismal life in Christ. He believes that time has order and significance because God is orchestrating the true course of history—from Creation and Fall, on to Incarnation and Redemption, finally to Second Coming and Final Judgment.

Yet this positive line has its negative counterpart, the legacy of evil. As we have seen, the demonic also embodies itself in specific individuals and events. The prophetic task of discernment, Mason teaches, is to identify the divergent lineages: the bright red line of salvation that is the boy's true legacy and the blurry dark arc of damnation that would cost the boy his soul. Accordingly, the elder Tarwater has instructed the younger in "two complete histories, the history of the world, beginning with Adam, and the history of the schoolteacher" (CW, 366). Old Mason has not schooled young Tarwater in the full ancestry of the world's evildoers, therefore, but rather in the roll call of biblical figures who have been imperiously summoned by God: "Abel and Enoch and Noah and Job, Abraham and Moses, King David and Solomon, and all the prophets, from Elijah who escaped death, to John whose severed head struck terror from a dish" (CW, 340). This list does not consist of those who were morally pure, but of a drunk and a doubter and a deceiver, a whiner and an adulterer and a schemer. As the maker and seller and consumer of contraband whiskey, Mason belongs in their line. Yet he has a profoundly biblical understanding of faithfulness. To be a Christian is not to become an ethically untainted person, much less a happily adjusted individual. To live faithfully is to become a person who dwells *coram Deo*—walking constantly before God—in repeated repentance and lifelong conversion.[17]

[17] This is Karl Barth's interpretation of Gen 17:1: "I am God Almighty; walk before me and be blameless." Cf. *Dogmatics in Outline*, trans. G. T. Thomson (New York: Harper Torchbooks, 1959), 49.

Like Jesus and the prophets, moreover, Mason Tarwater often retreated to the backcountry for direct engagement with the Lord. O'Connor's narrator reports that he would emerge from the woods looking "as if he had been wrestling with a wildcat." Like a latter-day Ezekiel, he was "full of the visions he had seen in [the wildcat's] eyes, wheels of light and strange beasts with giant wings of fire and four heads turned to the four points of the universe" (CW, 334). Whether in prophets ancient or modern, such dreadful confrontations cannot be discounted as the surfacing of mere subconscious fears.

Young Tarwater discerns this awful truth when the old prophet returns from one of his wilderness wrestlings with the Lord: "There was no fire in his uncle's eye and he spoke only of the sweat and stink of the cross, of being born again to die, and of spending eternity eating the bread of life" (CW, 334). Mason Tarwater is like Ezekiel in another regard. Whether the captive Israelites heed or spurn his message matters much less than that God's presence be decisively marked: "And they, whether they will hear, or whether they will forbear, (for they are a rebellious house) yet shall know that there hath been a prophet among them" (Ezek 2:5, KJV).

It is noteworthy that the elder Tarwater has not promised his great-nephew a life of prophetic glory or delight, but rather of pain and ignominy. Far from putting him on the road to American preacherly fame and success, the old prophet has called this stripling to a life of fearful suffering and sweated wrestling with God—indeed, to a holy violence: "He had schooled him in the evils that befall prophets; in those that come from the world, which are trifling, and those that come from the Lord and burn the prophet clean; for he himself had been burned clean and burned clean again. He had learned by fire" (CW, 332). The boy dreads a calling that would make him serve as a grounding rod for the divine lightning. He dreams, instead, of far more awesome feats of power: Moses striking water from a rock, Joshua making the sun stand still, Daniel staring down lions in a pit. Eager to perform such thrilling, even glamorous acts, the young Tarwater is disappointed that old Mason orders him to undertake the inglorious tasks of burial and baptism.

Satan as a Rebel Youth's Inner Voice

Young Tarwater looks forward to neither of his callings. When the old man dies, the boy labors for a day and a half at scooping out his great-uncle's grave. Yet gradually the gorge of rebellion rises within him, as the defiant youth finally abandons his spadework and heads off to the whiskey still, where his bootlegging great-uncle had manufactured not divine but earthly lightning, there to partake of alcoholic waters that will numb his conscience, while quenching neither his spiritual nor physical thirst.

Tarwater does not wage his spiritual war alone; he is also prompted by an inward interlocutor. My students were partially justified in reading this inner voice as the product of Tarwater's unconscious longings and frustrations, and thus as the boy's alter ego. As a thoroughgoing Thomist, O'Connor discerns the profound intersection of nature and grace, so that the human world is either elevated or degraded by its reception or refusal of the divine reality that bears down constantly upon it. Yet she leaves open another and more penetrating perception—namely, that this alien and intrusive speaker is the impersonator of Satan himself, the Tempter who operates not only by human permission but also by superhuman invasion. Here lies O'Connor's signal theological breakthrough: She depicts this subjective voice as arising not only from within the boy's own mutinous will, but also as assaulting him from without via satanic force.

Because young Francis Tarwater's conscience has been deeply formed by the religious teachings of his great-uncle, this Luciferian speaker at first seems strident and strange. Initially, the boy resents its insults against his dead uncle's life of prophecy. Old Mason had taught his great-nephew to have a deep reverence for the dead, the huge silent majority who constitute the authentic human *patria*. Not only did they literally parent us, but their rotted bodies also constitute the very *humus* beneath our feet, thus prompting, as the word suggests, a life of humility. "'The world was made for the dead. Think of all the dead there are,' [Mason] said, and then as if he had conceived the answer for all the insolence in the world, he said, 'There's a million times more dead than living and the dead are dead a million times longer than the living are alive'" (CW, 339).

Gradually, however, young Tarwater welcomes the inward interlocutor who enunciates the insolence the old prophet had condemned. It is the voice of theological rebellion, and it speaks with Dostoevskyan clarity about the relationship between parricide and deicide: If the boy can slay his immediate obligations to his dead great-uncle, he can rid himself of all other constraints as well. All things will be permitted, including wanton havoc: "'Now I can do anything I want to,' he said, softening the stranger's voice so that he could stand it. Could kill off all those chickens if I had a mind to, he thought, watching the worthless black game bantams that his uncle had been fond of keeping" (CW, 345). These are the accents of nihilistic autarky, even if they are given to a backwoods youth who has never heard of Friedrich Nietzsche or Ivan Karamazov. Once the demonic is permitted entrance, O'Connor shows, it assumes complete control. From having been an alien intruder, the devilish voice gradually becomes Tarwater's affectionate familiar:

> He didn't search out the stranger's face but he knew by now that it was sharp and friendly and wise, shadowed under a stiff broad-brimmed panama hat that obscured the color of his eyes. [The boy] had lost his dislike for the thought of the voice. Only every now and then it sounded like a stranger's voice to him. He began to feel that he was only just now meeting himself, as if as long as his uncle had lived, he had been deprived of his own acquaintance. (CW, 352)

Satan as Comic Fundamentalist

O'Connor's Devil is all the cannier for being a comic figure, much like the fiend in *The Brothers Karamazov*. He is a brittle rationalist and literalist who denies the bodily resurrection of the faithful dead on the grounds that many of them have been so thoroughly mangled that God could not possibly reconstitute their risen flesh into human form. "And lemme ast you this: what's God going to do with sailors drowned at sea that the fish have et and the fish that et them et by other fish and they et by yet others?" (CW, 352). This countrified Satan also argues—in accord with a good deal of late-modern politics and psychology—that young Tarwater's authentic selfhood depends on his complete independence and self-sufficiency. He must deny all divinely ordered authority in order to be free. And in complete accord with Baudelaire's dictum about demonic deception, Francis must learn to deny the Devil himself, especially when Satan denies his very own existence, as in the hilarious counsel he gives to the boy.

> The way I see it, [the inner voice] said, you can do one of two things. One of them, not both. Nobody can do both of two things without straining themselves. You can do one thing or you can do the opposite.
>
> Jesus or the Devil, the boy said.
>
> No no no, the stranger said, there ain't no such thing as a devil. I can tell you that from my own self-experience. I know that for a fact. It ain't Jesus or the devil. It's Jesus or you. (CW, 354)

As one who can quote Scripture, O'Connor's Devil proves brilliantly duplicitous. At first he seems indeed to be an orthodox theologian, denying that the incarnate Son of God can have Satan as his true opposite. In a certain sense this nefarious Spirit is also correct to aver that there "ain't no such thing as a Devil," insofar as it can be said that Lucifer has no proper existence, dwelling only in the unreality of non-being. Yet this latter-day Beelzebub's semblance of truth-telling soon ends. For in appealing to interior experience as the ultimate criterion for authenticity, he is a thoroughgoing subjectivist, one who locates truth only in the private and inward realm. Far more delusory is this cornpone demon's insistence that human flourishing stands in rivalistic competition with obedience to God: "It's Jesus or you." The central Christian claim is exactly to the contrary: Only by participating in the triune life of God through Christ and his Church, losing one's life for the sake of the Kingdom, does one find one's life (Mark 8:34–37). By contrast, the demonic life results in the absolute loss of God called hell.

The all-too-eagerly yielding Tarwater soon follows the command of his inner voice to abandon his gravedigging and to imbibe his great-uncle's self-made whiskey. At first, the satanic speaker recommends that the boy drink moderately, as if he were learning a well-mannered social practice; indeed, the wise-sounding demon recommends the golden mean in all things: "I wouldn't pay too much attention to my Redemption if I was you. Some people take everything too hard" (CW, 358). With every success in subduing the boy's will, the demonic voice ceases to sound less like an invasive stranger and more like Tarwater's alleged friend, indeed God's own advocate, urging him to take a "divine" draft of liquor to accomplish his own resurrection:

> Once you pass the moderation mark you've passed it, and that gyration you feel working down from the top of your brain . . . that's the Hand of God laying a blessing on you. He has given you your release. That old man was the stone before your door and the Lord has rolled it away. He ain't rolled it quite far enough, of course. You got to finish up yourself but He's done the main part. Praise Him. (CW, 359)

Young Tarwater soon becomes so thoroughly wasted with his great uncle's home-brew that he is able to "finish up" only by attempting the one thing that his dead uncle had strictly forbidden—the desecration of the old man's body by reducing it to ashes, burning down Powderhead on the assumption that the body of Old Tarwater is still inside it.

Young Tarwater's Flight to the City Where George Rayber Rules

It is altogether fitting that, when the fourteen-year-old Francis Tarwater abandons Powderhead in revolt against the fierce and sweated Christianity that the elderly prophet had taught him, he should flee his rural home to live in the city with his uncle George Rayber once again. Rayber is eager to give the boy Tarwater a crash course in civic life—its amenities as well as its responsibilities—so as to counteract the prophet's violently religious rearing of young Francis: "In four days they had been to the art gallery and the movies, they had toured department stores, ridden escalators, visited the supermarkets, inspected the water works, the post office, the railroad yards and the city hall. Rayber had explained how the city was run and detailed the duties of a good citizen" (CW, 397–98). The "natural" means of such civic salvation, as Rayber tells Tarwater, is "through your own efforts. Your intelligence" (CW, 451). "Baptism is only an empty act. . . . If there's any way to be born again," Rayber adds, "it's a way that you accomplish yourself, an understanding about yourself that you reach after a long time, perhaps a long effort. It's nothing you get from above by spilling a little water and a few words" (CW, 450–51). Thus does the school psychologist counsel the rebel anti-prophet with advice almost identical to that given by the satanic voice, even as he affirms, albeit negatively, the novel's main theme: "You want to avoid extremes," he tells the youth. "They are for violent people" (CW, 420).

Despite his cool counsel, George Rayber is consumed with a fiery anti-Christian zealotry, as he makes his own bitter assault on the Kingdom of God and what he regards as its sorry products. Like Ivan Karamazov, he is not an atheist so much as an anti-theist. Rayber believes that, if God exists at all, he is surely a Monster. Together with his Dostoevskyan predecessor, Rayber is determined to deny and refute this evil deity, this gnostic Demiurge. Rayber resembles Ivan in another way: He is not obviously demonic. On the contrary, he regards himself as a compassionate altruist. Believing his own life to have been blighted by the religious fanaticism of the old prophet, George Rayber has become a psychologist seeking to rescue other childhood victims of Christian fanaticism. Later in the novel, when Rayber overhears Lucette Carmody, a child evangelist, preaching at a tent revival, he sees her as yet another instance of the religious exploitation from which he must rescue such innocent creatures, returning them to his own humanist Eden:

> He had a vision of himself moving like an avenging angel through the world, gathering up all the children that the Lord, not Herod, had slain. . . . Rayber saw himself fleeing with the child [evangelist] to some enclosed garden where he would teach her the truth, where he would gather all the exploited children of the world and let the sunshine flood their minds. . . . Come away with me! he silently implored, and I'll teach you the truth, I'll save you, beautiful child! (CW, 413–14)

Can the Image of God in Man Be Destroyed?

O'Connor's novel poses an acute question: To what extent is Rayber so obsessed with a desire to serve as a secular savior that he himself becomes demonic? St. Athanasius warned that we can actually extinguish our humanity, effacing the image of God, returning to the nothingness from which we came. Hence his dire reference to "this dehumanizing of mankind, this universal hiding of the knowledge of [God] by the wiles of evil spirits."[18] St. Gregory of Nyssa also maintained that, when the divine image is completely destroyed, humans become demons. Is Rayber such a subhuman no-thing, a creature who becomes the Devil in disguise? O'Connor hints at such a possibility. Perhaps recalling that Lucifer is the former "angel of light," she names him Rayber, one who "bears rays."

Adrienne von Speyr illuminates this matter by describing what happens to the person who silences the divine summons by putting God off, as if the Lord of the cosmos could be made permanently to wait, so that we may do our own bidding rather than his. This negligent creature becomes a frightening figure, writes von Speyr, "a permanently marked man."

> He is and remains recognizable. He has pushed aside the experience of his life. In the future he remains embittered, dissatisfied, sarcastic, fault-finding, and he never grows tired of exposing his reasons, just concealing a sense of "knowing better" and trying to prove the impossibility of discipleship. But he is marked in advance; his words are superfluous.[19]

18 Athanasius, *On the Incarnation* (Crestwood, N.Y.: St. Vladimir's Seminary Press, 2002), 40.

19 Adrienne von Speyer, *They Followed His Call: Vocation and Asceticism*, trans. Erasmo Leiva-Merikakis (San Francisco: Ignatius Press, 1986), 31.

Rayber is this marked man. He can behold his own child with utter hardness of heart, as if he were a mangled mistake of nature, a biological botch. "His normal way of looking on Bishop was as an *x* signifying the general hideousness of fate. He did not believe that he himself was formed in the image and likeness of God but that Bishop was he had no doubt" (CW, 401). On at least one occasion Rayber has tried but failed to drown the "useless" Bishop. He also prophesies, quite accurately, that in future ages the birth of such "defective" children will be prevented; i.e., aborted or euthanized. Rayber's genuine-seeming humanism is thus characterized by a false and frightening nihilism. In his revolt against the violent witness made by the elderly prophet—who had kidnapped and baptized him as a child, confining him at Powderhead for an intense four-day catechesis—Rayber embodies a demonic violence of his own, as he seeks to deny all divine constraints upon his autonomous will.

Mason Tarwater, the Prophet Who Did Not Call Himself

Ironically, it is through George Rayber's anger at his prophet-uncle for placing the "curse" of Christianity on him that we discover the authenticity of Mason Tarwater's witness. As a school psychologist determined to expose his uncle as a religious fraud, Rayber approaches his scientific studies with alleged objectivity, dispassionately refusing to allow any ties of gratitude or familial regard to limit his research. In the name of "charity," therefore, he invited the ageing prophet to live in his home. Yet for the three-month duration of the old prophet's stay, Rayber had covertly analyzed him, observing all his actions and asking sly questions "that meant more than one thing, planting traps around the house and watching him fall into them" (CW, 331). Rayber's article, duly published in a scholarly journal, argued that the elderly prophet is a throwback to a primitive age, "a type that [is] almost extinct." In perhaps his most heartless act, Rayber asks the unsuspecting Mason to read the conclusion of his academic report: "This fixation of being called by the Lord had its origin in insecurity. He needed the assurance of a call and so he called himself" (CW, 378).

Mason Tarwater is enraged by this reductive reading of his holy summons—by Rayber's psychoanalytic contention that, subconsciously unable to accept his own insignificance, he invented his vocation in hope of divine grandeur. The aged preacher is convinced, on the contrary, that his prophetic witness springs from his painful encounters with the unknown and humanly unknowable God who has divinely identified himself in Israel and Christ. He complains, for instance, that Rayber the rationalist is cursed for not knowing that there are things he does not know. Mason remains angrily undaunted by Rayber's attempt to reduce his violent vocation to a pathetic psychological need.

> "Called myself!" the old man would hiss, "called myself!" This so enraged him that half the time he could do nothing but repeat it. "Called myself. I called myself. I, Mason Tarwater, called myself! Called myself to be beaten and tied up. Called myself to be spit on and snickered at. Called myself to be struck down in my pride. Called myself to be torn by the Lord's eye." (CW, 341–42)

For all his ranting, the old prophet goes to the heart of the universal Christian calling as Dietrich Bonhoeffer described it in his most celebrated single statement: "Whenever Christ calls us, his call leads us to death."[20] Rarely does the Christian life in the modern West constitute a summons to physical death by way of physical persecution; yet it remains a subpoena to die to one's own faithless presumption and to suffer the world's matching obloquy. Old Mason confesses that he has faced both kinds of violence—his conscience seared by divine judgment and his calling ridiculed by Rayber's contempt. Though no historian of modern culture, he boils with contempt for the Enlightenment idea of benign tolerance, based as it is on a fundamental division of body and soul—the omnicompetent nation-state governing all outward and public affairs from a supposedly neutral stance, while the churches allegedly attend to the inward and spiritual matters of the soul that pertain chiefly to the afterlife.

Just as reverence for mystery opens life to infinite possibility, so does repudiation of mystery produce a closed cosmos and a clamshell existence. It also reduces others to mere ciphers, to calculable units, to statistical numbers. Rayber's attempt to shrink the prophet's rich, complex, troubled life leaves old Tarwater feeling paralyzed, trapped, even mummified:

> For the length of a minute, he could not move. He felt he was tied hand and foot inside the schoolteacher's head, a space as bare and neat as the cell in the asylum, and was shrinking, drying up to fit it. His eyeballs swerved from side to side as if he were pinned in a

[20] Dietrich Bonhoeffer, *Discipleship*, trans. Barbara Green and Reinhard Krauss (Minneapolis: Fortress, 2001), 87. This is a more faithful rendering of "Jeder Ruf Christi fährt in den Tod" than Reginald Fuller's less literal but more dramatic version: "When Christ calls a man, he bids him come and die."

> straight jacket again. Jonah, Ezekiel, Daniel, he was at that moment all of them—the swallowed, the lowered, the enclosed. (CW, 378)

The elder Tarwater had learned the dire consequences of his unapologetic and intolerant faith when he was sent to a prison for the insane, there to serve a four-year sentence for abducting the child Rayber in order to baptize and catechize him. He could have been released much earlier had he been keen enough to recognize that his prophesying on the halls of the psychiatric ward served to prolong his incarceration. Yet the prophet's problem was not a mere lack of perception, as young Tarwater thinks. Like John Bunyan, Mason Tarwater possessed too much integrity to seek early release at the cost of his witness. His faith is as tough as an oak knot, and he is determined to fulfill his divine calling with biblical disregard for outward conditions. As a preacher of the Word, he is "instant in season, out of season" (2 Tim 4:2, KJV).

George Rayber as a Monk of Troubled Unbelief

Yet George Rayber is no atheist monster. Unlike Sheppard in "The Lame Shall Enter First," O'Connor depicts Rayber with compassion rather than contempt. He proves to be a rather pathetic impersonation of the Devil, if only because he is finally unable to maintain his frigid disregard for Bishop. Knowing well that old Mason has bequeathed to him an irresistible instinct for inward violence, Rayber lives a quasi-monastic life in order to master it. The school psychologist becomes a secular monk, ascetically depriving himself of the world's pleasures, lest they soften his stiff will not to believe: "He slept in a narrow iron bed, worked sitting in a straight-backed chair, ate frugally, spoke little, and cultivated the dullest for friends" (CW, 402). Rayber also refuses to deceive himself with happier alternatives, as if his vehement unbelief could make him blithely self-sufficient. With admirable clarity and honesty, he acknowledges that nihilism is the final alternative to Christianity. Thus has he determined to spend his life walking a tightrope of autonomous self-control, so that when he is finally forced to choose between the only two options—Belief and unbelief—he will elect a noble kind of nothingness:

> He was not deceived that this was a whole or a full life, he only knew that it was the way his life had to be lived if it were going to have any dignity at all. He knew that he was the stuff of which fanatics and madmen are made and that he had turned his destiny as if with his

> bare will. He kept himself upright on a very narrow line between madness and emptiness, and when the time came for him to lose his balance, he intended to lurch toward emptiness and fall on the side of his choice. (CW, 402)

Even if Rayber cannot believe, he remains a troubled unbeliever, unable to bask in his nihilist faith. Though he knows that his virtually mindless child will never (as the saying goes) "make a contribution to society," Rayber loves Bishop in his very uselessness, his stark gratuity: "It was love without reason, love for something futureless, love that appeared to exist only to be itself, imperious and all demanding." In fact, almost every created thing—precisely because of its otherness, its unnecessity, its sheer gift-character—can overwhelm Rayber with boundless charity: "Anything he looked at too long could bring it on. Bishop did not have to be around. It could be a stick or a stone, the line of a shadow, the absurd old man's walk of a starling crossing the sidewalk. If, without thinking, he lent himself to it, he would feel suddenly a morbid surge of love that terrified him—powerful enough to throw him to the ground in an act of idiot praise. It was completely irrational and abnormal" (CW, 401).

Rayber also fails to maintain his serene self-control when he hears the dying scream of Bishop as Tarwater drowns him. Having vowed to lurch toward nothingness when he is pushed to a final bitter choice, Rayber collapses instead. His breakdown may seem to indicate that he has at last succeeded in "putting God off," and thus that he is sinking into final death. Yet this scene is open to another and more positive reading. A truly nihilistic triumph of the Devil would surely have entailed Rayber's celebration, if only in an exhausted "tenderness," that useless Bishop is at last dead and that he himself can now live in peace. Rayber's collapse into unconsciousness may signal, on the other hand, the modest hope of O'Connor's extra-textual surmise: "He makes the Satanic choice, and the inability to feel the pain of his loss is the immediate result. His collapse then may indicate that he is not going to be able to sustain his choice" (HB, 484).

The reason for Rayber's potentially redeeming failure at the end is that the "madness" of divine charity does not have its counterpart in demonic emptiness, as if they were equals. The holy "violence" that old Mason had practiced on young Rayber—by baptizing and schooling him in the ways of prophecy during an intense four-day tutelage at Powderhead—is rooted in Reality as Rayber's election of the Void is not. Thus can he take no nihilistic pleasure in Bishop's death. His crumpling swoon is perhaps proof that George Rayber remains indelibly branded with the Cross, unable to remove its scarification any more than he can escape his own shadow. If so, he has experienced not a gruesome demonic victory but a blessed divine defeat.

The Holy Violence That Bears the Kingdom Away

As we have seen, the novel's two main perpetrators of holy violence are Mason Tarwater and his unwilling *protégé*, Francis Marion Tarwater. Yet both of them also practice a savagery that cannot be called sacred. Mason's brutality is negligible as compared to the cruelty of the younger Tarwater. Whereas the old prophet acts as Peter to Rayber's Malchus by virtually deafening him with a gunshot wound to the ear, his rebel successor has actually committed murder.

Flannery O'Connor chose not to narrate the novel's at once horrible and wondrous climax—wherein Francis Tarwater utters the baptismal formula even as he drowns Bishop—lest it seem mechanical and coerced, thus justifying the charge that her fiction is imbued with an heretically oppressive vision of reality.[21] Instead, she has Tarwater recall, well after the fact, what actually happened. This is the only way he can discover that he has been delivered from damnation at the same time he committed murder, his freedom being preserved rather than annihilated. Tarwater learns this paradoxical truth after hitching a ride with a truck driver who asks the youth to explain his soaked pants. Tarwater arrogantly replies that he has just finished drowning a boy. In one of O'Connor's most hilarious lines, the truck driver responds, "Just one?" Bishop's drowning is a joking matter for Tarwater as well, as he once again parrots Rayber's claim that baptism is a meaningless act and that we are born only once.

[21] The most hostile interpreter of this scene is the French critic André Bleikasten. He accuses O'Connor of being a procrustean author who has scripted the will of Francis Marion Tarwater into the service of a domineering deity, and who herself remained a misanthrope whose God is hardly distinguishable from the Devil: "O'Connor's heroes are indeed sleepers: they traverse life in a dream-like state, and with the sense of impotence and anxiety experienced in nightmares. They go through the motions of revolt, but their violent gestures toward independence are all doomed to dissolve into unreality. They are nothing more than the starts and bounds of a hooked fish. Tarwater and Motes both act out scenarios written beforehand by someone else" (André Bleikasten, "The Heresy of Flannery O'Connor," in *Les Americanistes: New French Criticism of Modern American Fiction*, ed. Ira D. Johnson and Christiane Johnson [Port Washington, N.Y.: Kennikat, 1978], 53).

Yet when the driver pulls off the road to sleep for a spell, the youth cannot avoid a dream-vision of what actually occurred as he and Bishop went boating on the lake bedside the motel where they were staying with Rayber. As if in solicitation of his baptism, Bishop had fixed his eyes on Tarwater and then crawled onto the boy's back, virtually urging a baptismal plunge, while Tarwater is standing by the boat in shallow water. Tarwater's demonic "friend" gives him nihilistic encouragement to "be a man" and to drown the dimwit. The dream-vision makes Tarwater a virtual spectator to his own act, as he is shown what he could not possibly recall through his self-interested memory. He sees with his inward eye and reenacts with his outward voice the undeniable truth: He has served as an agent of eternal life even as he caused an earthly death. "Suddenly in a high raw voice the defeated boy cried out the words of baptism, shuddered, and opened his eyes. He heard the sibilant oath of his [serpentine] friend fading away on the darkness" (CW, 463).

More profoundly than any other Flannery O'Connor interpreter, Rowan Williams goes to the heart of this troubling scene. Deeper still, he illumines O'Connor's entire theological vision:

> A God who fails to generate desperate hunger and confused and uncompromising passion is no God at all. It is not that Tarwater's life and faith are held up as a model of or for anything; they are what they are. And they are what they are because God is as God is, not an agent within the universe, not a source of specialised religious consolation. If God is real, the person in touch with God is in danger, at any number of levels. And to awaken the hunger that Tarwater at last recognises is to risk creating in people a longing too painful to bear or a longing that will lead them to take such risks that it seems indeed nakedly cruel to expose them to that hunger in the first place.[22]

A Satanic Sodomizing

Since a miracle was required to rescue young Francis from the clutches of his inward Satan as he simultaneously drowned and baptized the imbecile child Bishop, so is something akin to an anti-miracle required to deliver Tarwater from the spiritual grip of the Devil—namely, a sodomitic rape

[22] Rowan Williams, *Grace and Necessity: Reflections on Art and Love* (Harrisburg, Pa.: Morehouse, 2005), 118.

by "a pale, lean, old-looking young man" who had given the fleeing boy a ride. That O'Connor does not intend the nameless rapist to represent homosexuals as a class is made evident in his willfully caricatured features. He drives a lavender-tinted car, wears a lavender shirt, carries a lavender handkerchief, and possesses lavender eyes—the adjectival color being a standard symbol for decadence of all kinds, especially the sensual.[23] After drugging the boy into unconsciousness, the sodomite emerges from his (unnarrated) sexual violation of Tarwater as if he were a veritable vampire: "His delicate skin had acquired a faint pink tint as if he had refreshed himself on blood" (CW, 472).

Such a horribly anti-sacramental act, such a ghoulish feasting on Tarwater's semen, is a sign that that the image of God can indeed be effaced, as Athanasius declares, "by the wiles of evil spirits." No longer an inward voice, the Devil has assumed outward human likeness in a horribly violent and sexual manner. When the awakening Tarwater discovers the evil that has been perpetrated on him, he responds with appropriate apocalyptic fury:

> The boy's mouth twisted open and to the side as if it were going to displace itself permanently. In a second it appeared to be only a gap that would never be a mouth again. His eyes looked small and seedlike as if while he was asleep, they had been lifted out, scorched, and dropped back into his head. His expression seemed to contract until it reached some point beyond rage or pain. Then a loud dry cry tore out of him and his mouth fell back into place. (CW, 472)

This is a remarkable scene in nearly every way. It involves a literal demonic act at a time when the devil has largely disappeared from serious cultural and theological discourse. There is no other way to account for Tarwater's multiple assaults on the Gospel of Life except by identifying the Prince of Death, as O'Connor says, "with his specific personality for every occasion"—in this case, the occasion of Tarwater's at last being able to name the stranger who has been the catalyst for his evil deeds from the moment he first refused old Mason's call to a life of baptismal prophecy.

[23] It is noteworthy that the word "purple" is never used to describe the pervert, not only because it is not the same as "lavender," but also because it is the liturgical color of penitence.

The Violent Country Whose Silence Is Broken Only to Shout the Truth

In the boy's final driving out of the Devil, the legacy of the elder Tarwater has at last triumphed. Mason Tarwater remains O'Connor's chief exemplar of the holy violence that bears away the Kingdom. He is, in fact, her most convincing fictional portrait of the Christian life as a summons to make startling visible witness for Christ in the world. So it is with young Tarwater as well. It will not suffice for him to rout the evil visited upon him by the lavender-colored sodomite, though the youth seeks to purge the satanic presence by setting the woods afire. He must also confront the scene of his original betrayal. And so he heads home for Powderhead, expecting to meet the awful judgment that he deserves for having burnt—so he believes—the home and body of his great-uncle. The house indeed lies in ashes, but Buford, a black farmhand, had dragged the huge prophet from the burning house and given him the reverent burial the old man had ordered. To his immense astonishment and his even greater gratitude, young Tarwater finds that Buford has also laid the corn crop by and planted a crooked cross at the head of old Mason's grave.

This utterly unbidden and unmerited gift of grace, this act of sheer transcendent mercy that spares the youth a lifetime of overwhelming guilt, at last frees Tarwater to become the prophet he is meant to be. The flaming woods that he has set on fire no longer betoken the heat of the boy's anger but the ardor of God's summons: "He knew that this was the fire that had encircled Daniel, that had raised Elijah from the earth, that had spoken to Moses and would in the instant speak to him. He threw himself to the ground and with his face against the dirt of the grave, he heard the command. GO WARN THE CHILDREN OF GOD OF THE TERRIBLE SPEED OF MERCY" (CW, 478).

That prophets repent in sackcloth and ashes, abasing themselves in abject humility, does not make them immune from slaughter by the very people whom they are sent to save. In a letter commenting on Francis Tarwater's postfictional fate, O'Connor observed that "the children of God I daresay will dispatch him pretty quick" (HB, 342). Even if the boy-prophet dies while enacting his mission, his death will not invalidate his calling. He has seen what ultimately counts: The Cross is not a knife driven into the heart of the world; it is the true life-giving Tree—with arms sufficiently wide to embrace all the living, and roots sufficiently deep to encircle all the dead, as O'Connor herself said.

In the end, therefore, young Tarwater's vision reaches even to Paradise, for he is given a glimpse of Old Mason feeding eagerly among the great throng of the redeemed, as the multiplied loaf is passed among them. The boy knows that this hunger for the Bread of Life is also his, that it belongs not to him alone but to every living soul, and that no one can rest, as St. Augustine declared, until this craving is satisfied: "He felt his hunger no longer as a pain but as a tide. He felt it rising in himself through time and darkness, rising through the centuries, and he knew that it rose in a line of men whose lives were chosen to sustain it, who would wander the world, strangers from that violent country where the silence is never broken except to shout the truth" (CW, 478).

Conclusion

That O'Connor can envision the beatific realm as a "violent country" inhabited by violent men who are strangers on the earth reveals her abiding conviction that there are two kinds of violence, one earthly and the other heavenly. As we have seen, there are those who make a violent assault on the Kingdom by seeking to vacate it. They would replace our fumbling, struggling, but finally redemptive existence before God with a simulacrum. In the name of heedless autarky, the Raybers of this world would create an allegedly benign system wherein the scientific mastery of the physical order is violently applied to the moral order, if only with a mangling inward violence whose outward consequences become slowly but undeniably evident.[24]

That such a subhuman vision often passes as a true human accomplishment is proof, for Flannery O'Connor, that Satan has become both personally and culturally successful—indeed, that he is the world's unacknowledged prince and cause of its misery. His reign extends from the smallest personal sins to the Soviet gulags, the German crematoria, and the Chinese forced re-education camps, as well as our own destruction of Native Americans.[25] Hence her attempt, in *The Violent Bear It Away*,

[24] To treat human beings as impersonal objects having no transcendent *telos*, controlling and manipulating them for the alleged immanent good of earthly contentment, is to produce the greatest of calamities. Flannery O'Connor agreed with C. S. Lewis that such assaults on the Kingdom of God will end with the abolition of our very humanity: "Man's conquest of Nature turns out, in the moment of its consummation, to be Nature's conquest of man" (C. S. Lewis, *The Abolition of Man* [New York: Simon & Schuster, 1996], 76).

[25] Wendell Berry calls it the American Holocaust.

not only to name our pandemic demonry, but also to provide the final Alternative to it. There she has enabled readers to witness a salutary assault on the scandalous Kingdom as it is embodied in both Mason and Francis Marion Tarwater. They are indeed outrageous figures. Yet their offense lies not chiefly in the violence they visit on others but in the faithful ferocity they visit upon themselves. Only because they have been "torn by the Lord's eye" of divine judgment can they become baptismal prophets of divine mercy, bearing away the Kingdom of Heaven, not selfishly only for themselves, but also for whosoever else will come.

That Flannery O'Connor's drastic understanding of good and evil has large political implications requires that we examine her Augustinian politics.

6
Flannery O'Connor's Politics

On June 5, 2015, the U.S. Postal Service published a commemorative stamp in honor of Flannery O'Connor.[1] She was an anomalous candidate for such acclaim, since her work stands at a critical distance from the American project, both in its older and more recent iterations. Precisely in her refusal to assimilate her fiction to the national consensus, she made her most valuable gift to it.

The chief evidence for this claim is to be found in two 1963 issues of the Jesuit journal *America* that O'Connor read and marked only a few months before her death. In one essay, John Courtney Murray, the leading Catholic theologian on matters of Church and state at the time, expressed his hope that the Second Vatican Council's forthcoming treatment of religious freedom would be in full accord with what he called "the true political tradition of the Christian West." The American constitutional system, in Murray's view, has served to recover the Catholic rejection of all absolutisms, both ecclesial and governmental. It does so by insisting that "political authority has no part whatsoever in the care of souls (*cura animarum*) or in the control of the minds of men (*regimen animorum*)." Hence Murray's confidence that *Dignitatis humanae*, the Vatican II declaration on human freedom, would call for governments to remain secular and neutral by not according special privileges to any of the various religious traditions, but instead granting all of them freedom of both worship and belief.

Yet at the very end of his essay, Murray expressed a certain worry about this neat separation of spheres, whereby Church and state attend to their

[1] The first section of this chapter is taken from my essay, "Flannery O'Connor: Stamped but not Canceled," *First Things*, June 6, 2015, https://www.firstthings.com/web-exclusives/2015/06/flannery-oconnor-stamped-but-not-cancelled.

complementary and rarely conflicting affairs: "The question today is, whether the Church should extend her pastoral solicitude beyond her own boundaries and assume an active patronage of the freedom of the human person . . . who stands today under a massive threat to everything that human dignity and personal freedom mean."[2] Unlike Flannery O'Connor, Fr. Murray seemed impervious to the threats, both spiritual and physical, that might come from the American political system itself.[3]

The second essay, which O'Connor underlined and starred with asterisks, came from the young Jesuit theologian Bernard Coughlin, who argued a case much closer to O'Connor's own position. Fr. Coughlin warned that the American principle separating Church and state, when joined with our religious pluralism, becomes "a principle separating church and society." It confines Christian faith to the private sphere, as if it were an inward and invisible thing, when in fact it is an outward, visible, public Thing, as Chesterton properly capitalized it, an unabashedly communal and thus an irreducibly political reality. The Church's chief mission, therefore, is to worship the triune God and to practice its ethical life in full accord with its historic convictions. The Church is called to make prophetic witness, therefore, against all pretensions to secular autonomy. When the nation-state pretends to such sovereignty—as invariably happens—it is in fact no longer secular. It transforms itself into what Fr. Coughlin identified as "an antireligious religion." "To the Christian," he cautioned in June 1963, "secularism is a form of idolatry—the deification of man-made things."[4]

Flannery O'Connor resisted such idolatry. She gave her lasting fealty to Jesus Christ and his visible Church. She did not pledge her deepest allegiance to the flag of the United States of America nor to its national deity. This refusal makes her political vision thoroughly Augustinian. She configured both her personal and political loyalties via the *ordo amoris*, as St. Augustine named it, placing them in their proper hierarchy of greater and lesser goods.[5]

[2] St. Pope John Paul II would heed Murray's call for the Church to undertake "an active patronage of the freedom of the human person," especially in his signature encyclical, *Evangelium vitae* (1995).

[3] These quotations can be found in John Courtney Murray, S.J., "The Construction of a Christian Culture" (https://library.georgetown.edu/woodstock/murray/1940a).

[4] Quoted in Wood, "Flannery O'Connor: Stamped but Not Cancelled."

[5] I have dealt more extensively with O'Connor's politics in a review-essay on Jerome C. Foss' *Flannery O'Connor and the Perils of Governing by Tenderness*. It was published in *Interpretation: A Journal of Political Philosophy* 49, no. 3 (2023): 423–34.

The South as a Christ-Haunted and Bible-Saturated Region

Flannery O'Connor sought to embrace a distinctively Christian politics that would serve as a counterpoint to the regnant religion of the nation. She found it in her own place. Though too deeply acquainted with the griefs and horrors of Southern history ever to call her region Christ-centered, she saw that its terribly flawed people were still Christ-haunted: "Approaching the subject from the standpoint of the writer, I think it is safe to say that while the South is hardly Christ-centered, it is most certainly Christ-haunted" (CW, 861).

She also made this wry confession: "Whenever I'm asked why Southern writers particularly have a penchant for writing about freaks, I say it is because we are still able to recognize one." Southerners of O'Connor's sort possess unique antennae for detecting what is weird about all well-adjusted citizens of the world: "To be able to recognize a freak, you have to have some conception of the whole man, and in the South the general conception of man is still, in the main, theological" (MM, 44). Bible-permeated believers take the measure of themselves and others by the plumbline described by the prophet Amos (7:7–8). This True Vertical exposes all lateral deviations, whether left or right, political or religious.

Flannery O'Connor admired the virtues and lamented the vices of her region. Chief among the Southern virtues that made O'Connor a Roman Catholic at home among the folk Christians of the American South was their saturation in Scripture:

> The Hebrew genius for making the absolute concrete has conditioned the Southerner's way of looking at things. That is one of the reasons the South is a storytelling section. Our response to life is different if we have been taught only a definition of faith than if we have trembled with Abraham as he held the knife over Isaac. (MM, 202–3)

Her characters often tremble in terror, fearing that they too may be called to raise a blade over their own favorite sons. Thus are they perpetually freed from all political naivety.

> In the South the Bible is known by the ignorant as well [as the educated]. . . . When the poor hold sacred history in common, they have ties to the universal and the holy, which allows the meaning of their every action to be heightened and seen under the aspect of eternity. (MM, 203)

To view things *sub specie aeternitatis* is to envision their enormous capacity for both good and evil, and thus to be held in check from adopting easy schemes of political reform.

> What has given the South her identity are those beliefs and qualities which she has absorbed from the Scriptures and from her own experience of defeat and violation: a distrust of the abstract, a human dependence on the grace of God, and a sense that evil is not simply a problem to be solved, but a mystery to be endured. (MM, 209)

At least for Southern whites, the Civil War was an inglorious defeat in defense of a contemptible cause—slavery.

We have engaged Scripture aright, O'Connor concluded, when "like Jacob, we are marked" (MM 180). The Story of the world's creation and salvation is meant to mark and master us rather than for us to mark and master it. She admired the backwoods believers of the American South because they were biblically marked, even if not biblically mastered. Thus does she populate her fiction with gun-firing prophets and river-baptizing preachers. Her economically poor and educationally uncouth believers possess no cultural standing or political power; indeed, polite society has passed them by on the other side. She makes them the focus of her fiction not in scorn but sympathy.

A Southern Politics of Racial Injustice

Where could Flannery O'Connor find a faithful politics? Perhaps in American liberalism and its repudiation of the Jim Crow system of segregation and disenfranchisement, with its dreadful history of castrations and lynchings of black men? Odd though it may seem, the answer is a surprising No. The outrages visited by Southern whites on Southern blacks were not committed only, or perhaps even chiefly, by the folk Christians who populate her work. Jim Crow was an integral regime of law and violence, of beliefs and manners. It dominated the American South for three quarters of a century, beginning in the 1890s.

Yet it is seldom understood that such state-ordered racial apartheid was the creation of white elites. They sought to fortify the self-interested power that slavery once provided them. They of course welcomed poor whites into this political arrangement by offering them distinct racial prerogatives.[6] Yet the Jim Crow phenomenon found its broad appeal mainly

[6] The ideal of *noblesse oblige* called for the privileged ones at the top to treat the hapless ones at the bottom with both courtesy and charity. Yet there could be no fundamental breach of the system itself, even among whites. "Despite the many

within the white middle class. Lynch mobs were typically led not by the dispossessed, but by the most prominent white citizens.[7] This is not to deny that poor whites often profited from the Jim Crow system or that they participated in its race-baiting rituals, but simply to say that they were not its foundational source or driving force.[8]

The Vaporization of American Christianity

O'Connor's Augustinian politics is made evident in her contention that there was something ajar virtually from the outset of the American experiment. She lamented that, in his 1832 refusal to celebrate communion at First Church Boston, without first removing the bread and wine, Emerson began "the vaporization of religion in America" (HB, 511). The antisacramental church is the spiritual, the discarnate, the invisible church. Will Herberg noticed similar contradictions inherent in "the American way of life." The consensus religion of the nation was not, Herberg insisted, a careful distillation of deep theological commonalities lying at the core of Protestant, Catholic, and Jewish faith. It was "a secularized Puritanism, a Puritanism without transcendence, without [a] sense of sin or judgment." Instead, there was a felt religious need to sanction American wealth and success. Hence the appeal to such vague terms as "service," "stewardship," and "general welfare."[9]

---

provocations and depredations [that] rich white Southern men inflicted on poor whites," John Mayfield once rhetorically asked me, "how often did the latter lynch the former?"

[7] The murder of Emmitt Till in 1955 is perhaps the most obvious example. Richard Rankin Russell offers a powerful personal account of his own early life in the Delta region of northern Mississippi, where as a youth he heard jokes about the disposal of Till's riddled body in the Tallahatchie River until, as an adult, he came to confront its real horror. See "Down in the Delta: Tallahatchie County, Mississippi, and Langston Hughes's Blues Poetry about Emmett Till," *Five Points: A Journal of Literature and Art* 16, no. 2 (2014): 146–63.

The men who murdered young Till—Roy Bryant and his half-brother J. W. Milam—were not poor whites but middle-class property owners with considerable social standing. Byron De La Beckwith, the murderer of Medgar Evers, the Mississippi civil rights leader, was no redneck. He was educated at the prestigious Webb School in Bell Buckle, Tennessee.

[8] I owe this revisionist reading of Southern racial politics to my former student, John Hayes, especially his book, *Hard, Hard Religion: Interracial Faith in the Poor South* (Chapel Hill: University of North Carolina Press, 2017).

[9] Will Herberg, *Protestant—Catholic—Jew: An Essay in American Religious Sociology* (New York: Doubleday Anchor, 1955).

O'Connor also discerned the religious vacuity operating in the civic boosterism of the 1950s. An editorial in Henry Luce's *Life* magazine riled her because it charged that the nation's novelists, in their existentialist angst, were failing to celebrate their prosperous and optimistic country. Luce's editorialists summoned American writers to exhibit "the joy of life" and "the redemptive quality of spiritual purpose." Where was such joyful and redemptively religious purpose to be found? For Luce and his barkers, it lay in the nation's remarkable decade of success: its unprecedented wealth, its world-dominating military power, its virtual achievement of a classless society, at least in comparison with other nations. For Flannery O'Connor, when such purpose is located in economic prosperity, political power, and the like, it becomes idolatrous.

This is not to suggest that O'Connor was an ingrate concerning her American freedoms. She was critical of her country because she honored it. She regarded the threat of Soviet communism as so serious that she had a bomb shelter constructed on her Georgia property. O'Connor and her mother also welcomed a family of refugees from post-war Poland to work on their dairy farm. Their life at Andalusia became the occasion for one of O'Connor's finest stories, "The Displaced Person." O'Connor refused, in 1956, to sell her work to Czech and Polish publishers, lest they use it for anti-American propaganda, as they had done with Jack London's fiction. O'Connor also admired Reinhold Niebuhr for his stiff opposition to Khrushchev's Stalinist desire to remake the whole of humanity into *homo Sovieticus*. Despite the terrible limits of American self-assurance, it was immensely preferable to the mind-body-soul destroying politics of the Gulag Archipelago.

The "Wholesome," the Whole, and Life as the Will of God

Some of Flannery O'Connor's kinfolk complained about the predominance of grotesque characters in her work. They urged her to write about wholesome people. She replied that her characters are indeed whole because their peculiarity points, if often negatively, to a greater Wholeness. Like most biblical stalwarts, O'Connor's heroes are not good country people or just plain folks. They believe and they behave strangely. They often find what they are not looking for. They are put on the path toward something infinitely more important than social acceptance and economic prosperity. They are being burned clean and made whole—restored to the full, angular, thorny humanity that is in danger of being lost in our time. Together with C. S. Lewis, she feared that we are becoming people without chests—i.e., without the moral and religious sentiments of both heart and will that enable reason to rule the passions.

A people without chests is a sentimental people. Ours is an era when sentimentality has largely replaced sentiment, both politically and religiously. Brian Wilkie defines sentimentality as "a tender emotional response disproportionate to the situation, and thus [the substitution of] heightened and generally uncritical feeling for normal ethical and intellectual judgments."[10] Our sentimental political temptation is to believe that, because we can often repair human pain by human measures, we can also mend the human soul. For Chesterton, this amounts to total apostasy: "The huge modern heresy is altering the human soul to fit its conditions, instead of altering conditions to fit the human soul."[11]

Flannery O'Connor regarded sentimentality as nothing less than obscene when it envelops the Church:

> We lost our innocence in the fall of our first parents, and our return to it is through the redemption which was brought about by Christ's death and by our slow participation in it. Sentimentality is a skipping of this process in its concrete reality and an early arrival at a mock state of innocence, which strongly suggests its opposite. Pornography, on the other hand, is essentially sentimental, for it leaves out the connection of sex with its hard purposes and so far disconnects it from its meaning in life as to make it simply an experience for its own sake. (CW, 809)

Because she saw that sentimentality is to Christianity as pornography is to art, O'Connor was freed from a sentimental politics.

A Politics Neither Liberal nor Conservative

She could never espouse the liberal politics of an omnicompetent state because they often remain opaque to the human limits dramatized in the trembling fear and halting gait of her characters. Yet neither could she endorse the conservative politics that refuse all attempts to redress human misery via government-sponsored programs to relieve hunger and illness and poverty. Such conservatism is often rooted in the belief that life is essentially tragic and thus that political reforms are doomed before they are begun. "Naw," she starchily riposted, "I don't think life is a tragedy.

[10] Brian Wilkie, "What Is Sentimentality?" *College English* 28 (1967): 566.

[11] G. K. Chesterton, *What's Wrong with the World* (New York: Dodd, Mead, 1918 [1910]), 136.

Tragedy is something that can be defined by the professors. Life is the will of God and this cannot be explained by the professors; for which all thanksgiving" (CW, 928). O'Connor is not claiming that God wills everything that happens—thus making him the author of evil no less than good. She is maintaining, with Aquinas and the whole of orthodox Christianity, that nothing ultimately falls outside the divine purpose, even the ills he permits.[12]

Amidst the Age of Ashes and within the Culture of Death, divinely permitted evils have become almost unimaginable. At least 180 million people were murdered in the twentieth century alone—most of them by their own governments—more than in all previous centuries *combined*. Yet our divinely permitted freedom to pervert the Good is their source. We ourselves, not God, are to blame. Such hideous modern evils derive less—counterintuitive though it may seem—from a flint-hard *real politik* than from a softcore politics of tenderness. Hence Flannery O'Connor's most revolutionary pronouncement:

> In [our] popular pity, we mark our gain in sensibility and our loss in vision. If other ages felt less, they saw more, even though they saw with the blind, prophetical unsentimental eye of acceptance, which is to say, of faith. In the absence of this faith now, we govern by tenderness. It is a tenderness which, long since cut off from the person of Christ, is wrapped in theory. When tenderness is detached from the source of tenderness, its logical outcome is terror. It ends in forced labor camps and in the fumes of the gas chamber. (CW, 830–31)

O'Connor's fiction serves as a canary in the coal mine; it keels over when the oxygen runs low. Her life and work serve to alert our oxygen-starved culture and churches against a politics of tenderness. She saw, virtually from the start, that we Americans have undergone a gradual but almost tectonic shift in our character. The legitimate and hard-won freedoms of the Enlightenment, often beneficial to democratic states and confessing churches alike, are being construed as a call to refashion ourselves into whatever creatures we subjectively feel ourselves to be, thus devising a species drastically unlike anything previously known. Yet she also provided a politics capable of redressing our deadly pandemic.

12 I have dealt at length with the wondrous concurrence of human freedom and divine action in Ralph C. Wood, "G. K. Chesterton's Darkly Comedic Apologetics," *Logos* 27, no. 1 (2024): 57–81.

Conclusion

Flannery O'Connor helps free Christians from swearing uncritical allegiance to *any* political party or program. Conservative and liberal are not authentic theological but partisan political terms. Those who identify themselves via such terms usually adhere to the partisan politics of the right or the left, all the way down. Yet the visible Church is far from being an apolitical Church. It prevents us, perhaps surprisingly, from calling ourselves American Christians, if only by recalling that worshipers in Hitler's Church called themselves *Deutsche Christen*, German Christians. Rather should we identify ourselves as Christians in America. We are meant to embody the politics of the Kingdom of God in our prophetic and sacramental life. In Word and Sacrament, the audible and edible Church of Jesus Christ offers a drastically alternative politics to the best no less than the worst of all other regimes, transforming and reordering them all.[13]

Because an authentic Christian politics must be willing to embrace suffering, there is no better way to understand Flannery O'Connor's own encounter with irreducible suffering than in her friendship with Elizabeth Hester.

[13] I owe these crucial distinctions to my long-time friend and former colleague at Baylor, Barry Harvey.

7

Flannery O'Connor and Elizabeth Hester

A Friendship in Sacramental Suffering[1]

Flannery O'Connor was temperamentally disinclined to self-assertion, especially on social occasions, confessing that her function at her mother's tea parties was to cover the stain on the sofa. Yet in 1949 O'Connor could not restrain herself at a New York dinner party hosted by the ex-Catholic writer Mary McCarthy. As the hour grew late, McCarthy declared that she still found the Eucharist to be a useful symbol for her fiction, though of course she could no longer believe any of its hocus-pocus: "Well," declared O'Connor—to what must surely have been the astonishment of the other guests—"if it's a symbol, to hell with it."[2] In recounting this celebrated incident six years later, O'Connor made clear that she was not indulging in Catholic sanctimony: "That was all the defense I was capable of but I realize now that this is all I will ever be able to say about [the Eucharist] outside of a story, except that it is the center of existence for me; all the rest of life is expendable" (CW, 977).

American Christianity has been vaporous and invisible, as we have heard O'Connor complain, to the extent that it has been unsacramental. It has often lacked Christian substance because it has depended largely on pietism or moralism—on religious feelings or honorable deeds. The

[1] This chapter began as a plenary address at an Emory University conference on "The Prophet's Country: A Celebration of the Life and Work of Flannery O'Connor" in September 2007, when O'Connor's letters to Hester were first made public. I am grateful to Steve Ennis, the Director of the Manuscript, Archives, & Rare Book Library, for the original invitation as well as for the splendid hospitality that he and his colleagues at the Robert W. Woodruff Library provided me during my visit.

[2] "Having me there [at the party] was like having a dog present who had been trained to say a few words but overcome with inadequacy had forgotten them" (CW, 977).

result is that salvation is conceived in largely spiritual or ethical terms apart from life in the sacramental community. The Church itself is often understood, alas, as one organization alongside others that meet people's personal and social needs. The triune and incarnate God becomes a virtual hanger-on in such an operation.

In Elizabeth Hester, Flannery O'Connor found an unlikely companion in overcoming such fatal heresies. From the outset of their relationship, Hester had announced herself to be an atheist and had in fact called O'Connor a fascist (CW, 948, 951). This is an unpropitious beginning, to put it mildly, for a friendship that would become so deep and abiding that it would last for eleven years, until O'Connor's death in 1964. It is evident that O'Connor saw something not just humanly but also divinely promising in this unknown correspondent from Atlanta. Having met with blind consternation in many Christian as well as humanist readers, O'Connor rejoiced at discovering an unbeliever who saw that her fiction is God-drenched. "The distance [between us] is 87 miles," O'Connor begins, "but I feel the spiritual distance is shorter." "I would like to know," she concludes, "who this is who understands my stories" (CW, 942, 943). Elizabeth Hester could understand Flannery O'Connor's stories not only because she was intellectually keen and theologically astute, but also because she shared a history of suffering not unlike O'Connor's own.

The letters of O'Connor to Hester reveal the remarkable story of their friendship. They are the heart and soul of the Georgia writer's vast correspondence. O'Connor's letters are now regarded alongside Keats' as among the most significant in the entire Anglophone world. Aware that she was often pouring out her deepest concerns in them—and thus that they were likely to have lasting worth, many of her correspondents kept them. Thus can we be thankful that, in those antediluvian days before the internet and cell phones, O'Connor's chief venue for social existence was epistolary. For it was in these letters that O'Connor articulated her central concerns and there that she confessed the sacramental character of her faith.[3]

[3] Though there is a gathering body of work devoted to the sacramental quality of Flannery O'Connor's fiction, very little of it has been discerned in her letters. The most notable exceptions are Marion Montgomery, *Hillbilly Thomist*, 2 vols. (Jefferson, N.C.: McFarland, 2006); Susan Srigley, *Flannery O'Connor's Sacramental Art* (Notre Dame, Ind.: University of Notre Dame Press, 2004); Christina Bieber Lake, *The Incarnational Art of Flannery O'Connor* (Macon, Ga.: Mercer University Press, 2005); and John D. Sykes Jr., *Flannery O'Connor, Walker Percy, and the Aesthetic of Revelation* (Columbia: University of Missouri Press, 2007).

In Opposition Lies True Friendship

The blessed tie binding the lives of Elizabeth Hester and Flannery O'Connor was lashed with argument from beginning to end. They truly *engaged* each other in hospitable but vigorous disputation, thus justifying William Blake's celebrated saying: "Opposition is true friendship." It is important to note that, in her very first letter to Hester, O'Connor mentions suffering. It is as if she sensed that Hester's accusation that O'Connor was a fascist may have stemmed from her own suffering at the hands of the Church:

> I think that the Church is the only thing that is going to make the terrible world we are coming to endurable; the only thing that makes the Church endurable is that it is somehow the body of Christ and that on this we are fed. It seems to be a fact that you have to suffer as much from the Church as for it but if you believe in the divinity of Christ, you have to cherish the world at the same time that you struggle to endure it. (CW, 942)

In her direct epistolary witness to Elizabeth Hester no less than in the indirect witness embodied in her fiction, Flannery O'Connor is never an uncritical Catholic. On the contrary, she stresses her own limits and failings as a Christian: "I am not a mystic and I do not lead a holy life" (CW, 944). As a natal Catholic rather than a convert, moreover, O'Connor admits that "I am only slowly coming to experience things that I have all along accepted. . . . Conviction without experience makes for harshness" (CW, 949). "Smugness is the Great Catholic Sin," she adds later. "I find it in myself and don't dislike it any less" (CW, 983).

Flannery O'Connor's self-critical Catholicism helped make the atheist Elizabeth Hester not her enemy but her potential friend. Friendship is most often defined as shared devotion to particular goods, even to the point of laying down one's life for one's friends. This sentiment is known to pagans no less than to Christians. "Without friends," Aristotle declares in the opening lines of Book VIII, the celebrated section on friendship in the *Nicomachean Ethics*, "no one would choose to live, though he had all other goods."[4]

[4] *Nicomachean Ethics* 1155a, in *The Complete Works of Aristotle*, vol. 2, rev. Oxford trans., ed. Jonathan Barnes (Princeton: Princeton University Press, 1984), 1825. Aristotle also quotes Heraclitus' claim that opposition rather than likeness may serve as the basis for friendship: "'it is what opposes that helps' and 'from

There is another word in addition to the Greek φιλία that describes the Hester-O'Connor friendship. It is the Latin *fiducia*: abiding trust. That Flannery O'Connor introduced herself as a self-critical Catholic served to establish trust as the basis of their potential friendship. Though Flannery did not yet regard Betty as her friend, she saw that she could trust Hester to be truthful. "Truth" is in fact a word that originally connoted trust, fidelity, steadfastness—as in the wedding vow from Cranmer's Book of Common Prayer: "I plight thee my troth." Hester discerned a similar trustworthiness in O'Connor, if only because those whom one has labeled "fascist" do not often reply with a summons to friendship.[5]

In the *Rhetoric*, Aristotle also specifies the kind of activity entailed by φιλία as the highest kind of friendship. One desires for one's friend, says Aristotle, "what you believe to be good things, not for your own sake but for his, and [thus makes you] inclined, so far as you can, to bring these [good] things about."[6] It becomes clear, early in their correspondence, that Flannery regards Betty as such a friend—as one whom she desires to give the highest possible Gift insofar as she can offer it:

> This is a peculiar thing—I have the one-fold one-Shepherd instinct as strong as any, to see somebody I know out of the Church is a grief to me, it's to want him in with great urgency. At the same time, the Church can't be put forward by anybody but God and one is apt to do great damage by trying; consequently Catholics may seem very remiss, almost lethargic, about coming forward with the Faith. (Maybe you ain't observed this reticence in me.) I try to be subtle and succeed about as well as the gents in Washington Square . . . (HB, 134)[7]

---

different tones come the fairest tunes' and 'all things are produced through strife'" (1155b, p. 1826).

5 Soon O'Connor is forced to be blunt: "Find another word than fascist, for me and St. Thomas too. And totalitarian won't do either" (CW, 948).

6 *Rhetoric* 1380b36–1381a2, in Barnes, *Complete Works of Aristotle*, 2:2200. Yet Aristotle rules out all friendships with those who are "bad." "For the sake of pleasure or utility, then, even bad men may be friends of each other, or good men of bad, or one who is neither good nor bad may be a friend to any sort of person, but for their own sake clearly only good men can be friends; for bad men do not delight in each other unless some advantage can come of their relation" (*Nicomachean Ethics*, 1157a18–21, p. 1828). Such constraints are unacceptable to Christians, of course, who are commanded to love even our enemies (Matt 5:44; Luke 6:27).

7 The final reference is not to Henry James' novel, I suspect, but to the drag queens whom O'Connor had seen frequenting Washington Square during her brief

Christian Witness as an Invitation to All and Sundry

This remarkable confession—that O'Connor wants not only Hester but also her other non-Catholic friends to enter the Church—will strike many readers as strange, even offensive. In our late pluralistic age, almost everyone remains politely silent about such matters, as if one's religion were a private affair having no public and visible ramifications, certainly not anything one would allow to encroach on one's friendships. O'Connor anticipates the coming of privatized Christianity in the figure of Mrs. May in "Greenleaf." Upon discovering the white-trash woman named Mrs. Greenleaf prostrate over her mound of newspaper clippings, calling out for Jesus to heal the world's many miseries, Mrs. May winces: "She thought the word, Jesus, should be kept inside the church building like other words inside the bedroom. She was a good Christian woman with a large respect for religion, though she did not, of course, believe any of it was true" (CW, 506). Flannery O'Connor was convinced that the Gospel is indeed true, though not primarily private and intellectual. She regarded Christianity as an irreducibly public, visible, sacramental faith—a definitive communal way of life to which everyone may and must be invited.[8]

O'Connor responds stoutly to Hester's claim that, because so many of her characters come to the truth about themselves only in violent confrontations with death, she herself advocates the use of force:

> I am wondering why you convict me of believing in the use of force? It must be because you connect the Church with a belief in the use of force; but the Church is a mystical body which cannot, does not, believe in the use of force (in the sense of forcing conscience, denying the rights of conscience, etc.). I know all her hair-raising history, of course, but principle must be separated from policy. Policy and politics generally go contrary to principle. I in principle do not

---

stay in New York in 1949. They are not the butt of the joke, of course, but rather O'Connor herself.

[8] Emeritus Pope Benedict XVI shared this concern for Christian candor and truthfulness: "Only if the Christian faith is true does it concern all men; if it is merely a cultural variant of the religious experience of mankind that is locked up in symbols and can never be deciphered, then it has to remain within its own culture and leave others in theirs. That, however, means that the question about the truth is the essential question of the Christian faith as such, and in that sense it inevitably has to do with philosophy" (Joseph Cardinal Ratzinger, *Truth And Tolerance: Christian Belief and World Religions*, trans. Henry Taylor [San Francisco: Ignatius Press, 2004], 184).

> believe in the use of force, but I might well find myself using it, in which case I would have to convict myself of sin. . . . The only force I believe in is prayer, and it is a force I apply with more doggedness than attention. (CW, 951–52, 953)

Though O'Connor called herself a hillbilly Thomist, it is not obvious how Aquinas' theology shapes O'Connor's religious vision. Her fiction often appears to embody a Jansenist if not Manichean opposition between nature and grace. Her characters come to recognize their need for salvation only through violence, usually in the moment of death, whether as the Grandmother faces The Misfit's gun barrel in "A Good Man Is Hard to Find" or as Mrs. May confronts the charging bull in "Greenleaf." Such drastic clashes seem far removed from the Thomistic conviction that divine grace does not negate and destroy but completes and perfects both the human and the natural realms according to what is already latent in them, even after the Fall.

Frederick Bauerschmidt points out that we have misread Aquinas in thinking that the nature-grace relation constitutes a seamless unity having no tensions or stresses. On the contrary, Bauerschmidt contends, Aquinas discerns grace as perfecting the human only by first prompting "us to reach out beyond the confines of our nature." "[F]or just as form perfects matter by stirring it to act, 'troubling' and 'goading' it into actuality, so too grace perfects nature by disturbing it."[9] O'Connor's characters are not coerced, therefore, so much as they are troubled into a proper response to God. Far from having salvation thrust on them perforce, they finally cooperate with the grace that has been preveniently goading them throughout their lives.

Nihilism as the Perennial Counter-Evidence against Belief in God

The Church's invitation to become friends of God can never bypass the massive counter-evidence against faith in God. That the cosmos seems both accidental and pointless, having only the order that the ruthless and powerful impose on the weak and cowardly, was a notion that O'Connor could not dismiss out of hand. The daily bulletins from Hell delivered by social media are sufficient evidence to make one fear what Hulga Hopewell espouses in "Good Country People" (There's nothing but Nothing) as well

[9] Frederick Christian Bauerschmidt, "Shouting in the Land of the Hard of Hearing: On Being a Hillbilly Thomist," *Modern Theology* 20, no. 1 (2004): 176.

as what Hazel Motes preaches in *Wise Blood* ("There's no truth behind all truths").[10] "In or out of the Church," O'Connor confesses to Hester, nihilism "[is] the gas you breathe" (CW, 949).

The chief temptation of nihilism is to employ force in order to accomplish self-devised goods. There being no transcendent order by which human desires might be reordered to the Good, we must both devise and enforce our own schemes for human betterment. While remaining open to "just war" sanctions for the use of outward force, O'Connor makes clear that there can be no ecclesial acts of moral or spiritual compulsion. For her, the Gospel is the ultimate Invitation, and thus a matter always of attraction and persuasion, never of coercion. Flannery thus urges Betty to enter the Church only if her conversion is not forced, only as it serves as an enlargement, not a diminishment, of her freedom:

> This is what you are doing and you are right, but do not make your feeling of the voluptuous seductive powers of the Church into a hard shell to protect yourself from her. I suppose it [coming into the Church] is like marriage, that when you get into it, you find that it is the beginning, not the end of the struggle to make love work. (6 August 1955)[11]

Having exhibited such startling candor and humility in making Christian witness to her friend, O'Connor can hardly be accused of leading Hester into the Church as if the Body of Christ would resolve all her troubles, whether personal or intellectual. They both struggled to set their friendship on a basis that would avoid all easy affirmations—i.e., on a trust that, though it takes human form, has its origin and sustenance in the God who has entrusted himself to the world.

[10] Motes' cornpone nihilism may derive more from O'Connor's reading of Jean-Paul Sartre than Friedrich Nietzsche. Sartre argues that human consciousness overreaches its animal limits when it attains self-consciousness. According to Sartre, such a mental vault does not constitute a burst into full humanity but a leap into the Void. Hence his celebrated definition of humanity as a "sorry project"—an accidental thing absurdly thrown into existence.

[11] This and all other previously unpublished letters were copyrighted by the Mary Flannery O'Connor Charitable Trust in 1955 and 1956, then renewed in 1983 and 1984 by Regina Cline O'Connor. The Trust has granted permission to cite them, while all rights remain reserved.

Conversion as God's Unique Gift

O'Connor's letters reveal that she regarded herself as Betty's secret spiritual advocate long before she became her open baptismal sponsor. Nor as her unofficial tutor did Flannery seek to distinguish among the various theological strands of contemporary Catholicism but rather to emphasize the gravamen and essence of the Faith that she herself had both received and embraced. It all centers on the nature of conversion and the struggle that it entails. Knowing well that faith is always a divine gift, O'Connor scrupulously avoids any ownership of Hester's entrance into the Church. On the contrary, she expresses astonishment at the news: "To my credit it can be said anyway that I never considered you unbaptized. . . . All voluntary baptisms are a miracle to me and stop my mouth as much as if I had just seen Lazarus walk out of the tomb. I suppose it's because I know that it had to be given me before the age of reason, or I wouldn't have used any reason to find it" (CW, 982).

How, then, do such conversions of the recalcitrant human heart and mind occur? Not, O'Connor makes clear, by the promise of reward, as if embracing the Gospel meant the redress of previous damages and the guarantee of freshly-won benefits. Rather than providing a satisfactory new life, authentic conversion often entails painful deprivation and suffering: "Some kind of loss is usually necessary to turn the mind toward faith" (HB, 159). It also entails the Pauline confession of Colossians 1:24: "Now I rejoice in what I am suffering for you, and I fill up in my flesh what is still lacking in regard to Christ's afflictions, for the sake of his body, which is the church." St. Paul does not deny that Christ bled and died and rose for all who believe; he calls, instead, for Christians to "fill up" the afflictions that Jesus did not bear in his earthly ministry by suffering for others, perhaps especially for those who do not or perhaps even cannot believe, indeed for souls such as Elizabeth Hester.

The Summons to Self-Surrender

The longer one peruses Flannery O'Connor's letters to Betty Hester, both before and after Hester called herself a Christian, the more it becomes evident that Christian faith has one requisite above all others—namely, the gift of total self-surrender, an unstinting willingness to participate in the suffering of Christ for the redemption of the world. It is a privilege that baptismal grace lays on cradle Christians no less than new believers. It is not an act performed once and for all; rather does it require continual, daily reconversion.

In O'Connor's case, such participation in the suffering of Christ entailed not only the acceptance of an illness that would lead to her early death, but also a return to the confining circumstances of rural Georgia life under the care of her mother, when she had hoped to live at a critical distance from the South while writing about nothing else. She was thus required to surrender all hope for an ordinary existence. That she would never marry or have a life that she could call her own became the inexorable if painfully embraced fact:

> You are wrong that it was long ago I gave up thinking anything could be worked out on the surface. I have found it out, like everybody else, the hard way and only in the last years as a result of I think two things, sickness and success. One of them alone wouldn't have done it for me but the combination was guaranteed. I have never been anywhere but sick. In a sense sickness is a place, more instructive than a long trip to Europe, and it's always a place where there is no company, where nobody can follow. Sickness before death is a very appropriate thing and I think those who don't have it miss one of God's mercies. Success is almost as isolating and nothing points out vanity as well. But the surface hereabouts has always been very flat. I come from a family where the only emotion respectable to show is irritation. In some this tendency produces hives, in others literature, in me both. (CW, 997–98)

Never does O'Connor downplay the difficulty of such willingly-borne sacrifice. In one of her most poignant letters to Betty, Flannery acknowledges that, as a speaker at meetings of the American Legion,[12] her father found a challenging life beyond the confines of his daily routine: "He needed the people I guess and got them. Or rather wanted them and got them. I wanted them and didn't. We are all rather blessed in our deprivations if we let ourselves be, I suppose" (HB, 169). The heart of this moving confession lies in its two drastic qualifiers: "rather" and "suppose." She is *rather* blessed for accepting her losses, she *supposes*. Or as O'Connor said in early and wrenchingly honest admission to Elizabeth and Robert Lowell soon after her return to Milledgeville: "I have enough energy to write and as that is all I have any business doing anyhow, I can *with one eye squinted take it all as a blessing*. What you have to measure

[12] Ed O'Connor served as Commander of the American Legion for Georgia, and young Flannery traveled with him as he gave speeches across the state.

out [in small portions], you come to observe closer or so I tell myself" (CW, 910, emphasis added). Once again, the real reservations—namely, the skeptically narrowed eye and the partially convinced self-reminder. Writing to Hester in just her second letter, O'Connor is still more candid: "When I ask myself how I know I believe, I have no satisfactory answer at all, no assurance at all, no feeling at all. I can only say . . . Lord I believe, help my unbelief. And all I can say about my love of God, is, Lord help me in my lack of it" (CW, 944).

Personal Transformation via Purity and Participation in the Sufferings of Christ

The heart of conversion from unbelief to belief, by way of repeated acts of self-surrender, is personal transformation—the slow but permanent reordering that constitutes the Christian life. The New Testament word for repentance and conversion is *metanoia*. It indicates a radical reversal, an utter about-face, an entire redirection of one's life-course, and thus a total change of mind. It seems evident from their earliest exchanges that Elizabeth Hester wants to probe this question of *metanoia*: To what extent will Betty be changed, if at all? With keen spiritual sensitivity, O'Connor links Hester's suffering to *purity*. It is not only or even chiefly a sexual virtue, as if the virginal innocence of a pre-pubescent child exemplified it. "Purity," Flannery declares to Betty in an early letter, "strikes me as the most mysterious of the virtues and the more I think about it the less I know about it" (CW, 970).

O'Connor illustrates the relation of repentance and conversion to purity of heart by answering Hester's query concerning the nameless hermaphrodite in "A Temple of the Ghost." He is a seemingly pathetic creature who survives by exhibiting his sexually mixed features to gawkers at carnivals, thus enabling such voyeurs to delight that they are not as he is. Yet, as we have heard, the hermaphrodite repeatedly affirms his wretched condition by declaring that "God made me thisaway and if you laugh He may strike you in the same way. This is the way He wanted me to be and I ain't disputing His way. I'm showing you because I got to make the best of it" (CW, 206).

Flannery cannily though implicitly links the hermaphrodite's embrace of his wretched state to Betty's own summons to Christian faith: "As near as I get to saying what purity is in this story is saying that it is an acceptance of what God wills for us, an acceptance of our individual circumstances"

(CW, 976).[13] Such self-abnegation entails neither cringing submission nor careless passivity. On the contrary, corporal and spiritual works of mercy constitute the core of the Christian life: "Resignation to the will of God," O'Connor writes, "does not mean that you stop resisting evil or obstacles, it means that you leave the outcome out of your personal considerations. It is the most concern coupled with the least concern" (HB, 419).

This arduous, passionate, lifelong transformation is not a bleak and grim business but the supremely joyful life. It entails the proper ordering of our loves to the love of God, renouncing lesser goods for greater. Unsullied faith is thus akin to true humility: To possess it is to be unaware of it. "On the matter of purity we can never judge ourselves," O'Connor affirms to Hester, "much less anybody else. Anyone who thinks he's pure is surely not" (CW, 978).[14] Repeatedly, therefore, O'Connor describes conversion as radical participation in the life and death of Christ. As we have seen, Flannery does not ask Betty to undertake a struggle that she has not undergone herself. Though the Christian life has brought happiness to O'Connor in the ultimate sense, it has cost her in the immediate term.

Elizabeth Hester's "Horrible History"

We do not know precisely what Elizabeth Hester confessed to Flannery O'Connor about her own identity except that it concerned what O'Connor calls Hester's "horrible history" (CW, 994). Betty's grievous past included the father's abandonment of both his daughter and wife, the suicide of Hester's mother in the thirteen-year-old girl's presence, as well as Betty's own abandonment by a lover with whom she had eloped. It also encompassed Hester's enormous frustration as a lonely intellectual confined to mind-numbing work in a retail credit office. Nor is there any doubt that Betty's unhappy life story entailed her dishonorable discharge from the U.S. Air Force because of her uncloseted lesbianism.

[13] The Catholic Catechism locates purity not in the loins but the heart as "the seat of moral personality," even as the Beatitudes declare that "Blessed are the pure in heart, for they will see God." The Catechism also teaches that the "pure in heart are those who have attuned their intellects and wills to the demands of God's holiness in charity, chastity, and love of truth."

[14] "Now it was the inmost lie of the Manichees that they identified purity with sterility. It is singularly contrasted with the language of St. Thomas, which always connects purity with fruitfulness; whether it be natural or supernatural" (G. K. Chesterton, *St. Thomas Aquinas: The Dumb Ox* [Garden City, N.Y.: Doubleday Image, 1956 (1933)], 109).

O'Connor responds to Hester's apparent admission that she is a lesbian by admitting her own failures in charity while also promising nothing but charity toward Betty herself: "I have a tendency . . . to dismiss other people's torments out of hand, but this one, being yours, will have to be partly mine too. It only hurts me because it has hurt you and inasmuch as the temporal effects can still hurt you now." Betty apparently feared that her long-delayed disclosure might mean an end to their friendship, as if O'Connor would let Hester simply "drop out of my existence." Flannery answers such delusion by professing the *philia* that is at once human and divine:

> It would be impossible for me to let you [thus disappear]. You have done me nothing but good and you have given me the present you wanted to, but the fact is, above and beyond this, that I have a spiritual relationship to you; I am your sponsor, self-appointed from the time you first wrote me and appointed by you afterwards, which means that I have a right to stay where I've been put. I can see how very much grace you have really been given [Flannery concludes] and that is all that is necessary for me to know in the matter. What is necessary for you to know is my very real love and admiration for you.[15]

Flannery O'Connor's quiet acceptance of Betty Hester's lesbianism is remarkable in several ways. Perhaps the most obvious is that Flannery has no prying curiosity, no desire for lubricious details. On the contrary, she treats the question with an admirable objectivity, making clear that their friendship is not in jeopardy. Yet while she refuses righteously to condemn Betty, neither does she sentimentally sympathize with her for wanting to be a practicing homosexual. Flannery thus avoids the language of victimization, even though conventional gender boundaries had done Betty considerable harm. Instead, O'Connor reads her friend's condition in theological terms, commending Hester for acknowledging her sexual propensity as well as for paying the price it exacted—calling her to suffer not for her own sake but for God's.

We Are More Than Our History

O'Connor acutely discerns that self-acknowledged guilt is not the key to Hester's potential conversion and transformation. So long as she remains sunk in self-reproach, she cannot be free. Self-accusation can always

15 October 31, 1956.

be answered with self-justification. Flannery thus summons Betty to a more excellent way, a way for her to be neither defined nor confined by her lesbianism. Thus does Flannery direct Betty to the divine means for becoming the person she is meant to be. "What you have to accept now," O'Connor graciously insists, "is the forgiveness [of God] and I daresay that is harder to accept [than shame and remorse] and that you have to do it over and over."[16]

Mercy, not guilt, constitutes the core of the Gospel. Counterintuitive though it seems, Flannery sees that God's grace will be exceedingly difficult for Betty to embrace. Bondage seems paradoxically preferable to liberty, since the greatest of all Gifts entails the greatest of all privileges and responsibilities. Forgiveness flings wide the cell door, leaving the prisoner to walk free. No longer in flight from the law, the ex-convict is now at large to live a transformed life. "Love God," said St. Augustine, "and do what you will." In an especially important letter, O'Connor succinctly summarizes the nature of salvation. "The meaning of the Redemption," she tells Hester, "is that we do not have to be our history and nothing is plainer to me than that you are not your history." In a subsequent letter, Flannery slightly modifies this claim by encouraging Betty to remember that "you are more than your history. I don't believe that the fundamental nature changes, but that it's put to a different use when a conversion occurs and of course it requires vigilance to put it to the proper use" (HB, 184).

That a bodily or spiritual condition is inherited rather than chosen does not make it inherently commendable. An inborne and abiding proclivity for anger—a wrathful impatience with the world's failure to do one's own bidding—will produce a life of destructive fury unless it is transformed into zeal for the good. O'Connor does not urge Hester to cease being a lesbian, therefore, nor does she promise easy freedom from her miserable past. Betty will remain, to no small extent, the person whom her genetics and her "horrible history" have made her. Her entry into the Church will not mean that her wretched life story will be forgotten or ignored so much as confronted and redeemed. So will her sexual orientation not be reversed but redirected toward redemptive ends—perhaps through *homophilia*, in friendships such as Flannery and Betty themselves enjoyed.

[16] October 31, 1956.

Apostasy as a Lessening of the Desire for Life

It is noteworthy that Flannery O'Connor expressed worry about her friend's faith long before Hester left the Church in 1961. In a letter to the writer John Hawkes, she voices her distress over Betty's lack of a real outlet for her considerable talent: "A. does seem to kill off her energy when she writes fiction, but it pains me to see this much intelligence with nothing to do with itself" (CW, 1150). More pertinent, in retrospect, is Flannery's constant recourse to the topic of conversion—as if to remind Betty that drastic mercy entails drastic judgment: "This notion that grace is healing omits the fact that, before it heals, it cuts with the sword Christ said he came to bring" (HB, 411). Yet again: "I don't know if anybody can be converted without seeing themselves in a kind of blasting annihilating light, a blast that will last a lifetime" (HB, 427). Most prophetic of all, perhaps, is O'Connor's caveat that Betty's entry into the Church will not entail a singular, punctiliar change but a continual, repeated deepening of her moral life:

> I don't think of conversion as being once and for all and that's that. I think once the process is begun and continues that you are continually turning inward toward God and away from your own egocentricity and that you have to see this selfish side of yourself in order to turn away from it. I measure God by everything that I am not. I begin with that. Maybe this depends on the person and is different for different people. (CW, 1144)

The softening qualifier at the end may reveal that, though she wants to avoid hectoring, O'Connor fears that Hester may be unable to sustain her initial conversion.

Betty's announcement, five years later, of her departure from the Church proves deeply saddening to Flannery and her mother:

> I don't know anything that could grieve us here like this news. I know that what you do because you think it is right. I don't think any the less of you outside the Church than in it, but what is painful is the realization that this means a narrowing of life for you and a lessening of the desire for life. Faith is a gift, but the will has a great deal to do with it. The loss of it is basically a failure of appetite, assisted by sterile intellect. . . . But let me tell you this: faith comes and goes. It rises and falls like the tides of an invisible ocean. If it is presumptuous to think that faith will stay with you forever, it is just as presumptuous

> to think that unbelief will [also stay forever]. Leaving the Church is not the solution. (CW, 1152–53)

By "a lessening of the desire for life," O'Connor does not suggest that Hester will be deprived of her *joie de vivre*, but that she will inhabit a smaller sphere of reality. As Frederick Bauerschmidt acutely comments on this exchange, "In losing that which is beyond our nature, we lose our nature."[17] Hester will still have her human life, but she will have lost her life as a creature dwelling redemptively in the presence of God. Even so, Flannery the believer seeks to remain patient with Betty the ex-believer.[18]

Two weeks after the news of Betty's departure from the Body of Christ, O'Connor cautions Hester that her increased self-confidence will confine her to a shrunken realm, one limited only to those things that she can comprehend: "I see that I was wrong in my speculation that you would have even less confidence in yourself. You have more, of course. Faith is blindness and now you can see. Faith is an over-reaching; now what you reach for is within your grasp" (CW, 1154). Two years later, O'Connor warns Betty that she has forfeited her ethical focus. "Your views on morality," Flannery tartly declares, "are for never-never land. We don't live in it" (HB, 526). Perhaps the key to Hester's lapse lies in O'Connor's discernment that her dear friend has seriously misread the meaning of self-abandonment to God:

> What I [. . .] wonder at is that you were in the Church five years and came out with such a poor understanding of what the Church teaches—that you confuse self-abandonment in the Christian sense with a refusal to be yourself, with self-torture. . . . Accepting oneself does not preclude an attempt to become better. It is, in fact, primary to that effort as the Church has always taught. Self-torture is abnormal; asceticism is not. (HB, 457–58)

By becoming "better" O'Connor does not intend anything akin to self-improvement. Hester was meant, instead, to embrace the love of God

17 Bauerschmidt, "Shouting in the Land of the Hard of Hearing," 176.

18 There is nothing so scorching, for instance, as O'Connor's response to Robert Lowell's announcement that he had left the Church: "That you are not in the Church is a grief to me and always has been and will be and I know no more to say about it. I severely doubt that you will do any good to anybody 'outside' as you call it, but it is probably true that you will do good for yourself in as much as you will be the only one in a position to" (CW, 924).

within the constraints of her sorrowful history. Her new baptismal life was not designed to deny her sexual and personal suffering—her history of unhappiness—but to free her from being shackled by it. Taking up and bearing the Cross is not a perverse kind of self-scourging, as Hester came to believe. Rather does it require a radical reordering of our desires, redirecting even the most clamant inclinations to the highest of ends, the love of God.

A Flight from the Body into Abstractions

That Hester had made a theological more than a moral act of apostasy becomes ever more evident. Flannery had warned Betty that, as one inclined to the abstract over the concrete, she would be tempted to dwell in the stratosphere of pure ideas, ungrounded notions, wandering convictions unmoored from ecclesial reality. Thus have we heard O'Connor declaring that Hester's loss of faith "is basicly a failure of appetite" (CW, 1153). This is a straightforward Thomistic caveat. "Appetite" does not mean physical hunger, of course, but a desire for the good. Nor is "intellect" to be understood as calculative thinking so much as perception and understanding of the good. The right use of intellect issues, not in mere moral reform, but in the fulfillment and realization of our proper end. Having forsaken the sacramental life for an anti-sacramental existence, Hester will become ever less fertile, ever more barren, in her thinking. O'Connor laments this loss in a letter to Cecil Dawkins:

> I'll tell you what's with [Betty], why all the exhilaration. She has left the Church. Those are the signs of release. She's high as a kite and all on pure air. The conversion was achieved by Miss Iris Murdoch, as you could doubtless see by that paper [presumably, an essay by Hester]. [Betty] now sees through everything and loves everything and is a bundle of feelings of empathy for everything. She doesn't any longer believe that Christ is God and so she has found that he is "beautiful! beautiful!" Everything is in the eeeek eeek eureka stage. The effect of all this on me is pretty sick-making but I manage to keep my mouth shut. I even have restrained myself from telling her that if Christ wasn't God he was merely pathetic, not beautiful. And such restraint for me is something! . . . She thinks she's at last discovered how to be herself and has at last accepted herself. She says she's always tried to be somebody else because she hated herself, but now she can be herself. It's as plain as the nose on your face that now she's

> being Iris Murdoch, but it is only plain to me, not her. What I am afraid of is that the reaction is going to set in in a couple of months, or maybe not that soon, but sometime, and when it does BANG. Everything runs to extremes with her, as you can see. (HB, 459–60)

O'Connor's dire prophecy of Hester's eventual suicide is not the most signal aspect of this searing analysis. Flannery does not fear that Betty has let her lesbianism trump her faith. Hester possessed too much ethical integrity to find refuge in hedonic pleasure. She may have had occasional infatuations, but she would never resort to serial lovers. Instead, she would continue to share a one-bedroom apartment with her elderly aunt, Mrs. Gladstone Pitt, living much as she had all along—chain-smoking, sleeping on the couch, surrounded by mounds of books. O'Connor sees that the problem lies not with a self-indulgent sexuality but with Hester's conviction that she has discovered "how to be herself." For in "being Iris Murdoch,"[19] Hester has rejected the Scandal that could have made her more than her sexual history. Betty wanted, albeit paradoxically, also to escape her body. She sought to become a pure soul.

Responding to Plato's argument that the soul constitutes our immortal essence, Aquinas declares that the soul does not merely inhabit the body as sailors dwell in ships or even as people wear clothes—namely, as something merely incidental to it. On the contrary, Aquinas claims that "being alive is existing as a living thing," in an inseparable unity of body and soul. To deny the necessity of the body for the soul is to deny that we are finite creatures. "So the soul is that by which the human body actually exists. . . . So the human soul is the form of the human body." In a remarkable conclusion that flies in the face of Murdoch and Hester no less than Plato, Aquinas concludes that "soul is not the whole human being, only part of one: *my soul is not me*."[20] So intrinsic is the body to the soul's perfection, in fact, that the soul's final and complete fullness will be found only in the resurrected body.

Flannery O'Connor sought to lead Elizabeth Hester toward a saving regard for her own body and its sexual suffering. Thus does she offer acute theological discernment in reply to Hester's complaint that she

19 The two women were in fact to correspond for thirty years, their letters ending only with Murdoch's descent into Alzheimer's in the mid-1990s; she died in 1999. Murdoch had a high regard for Hester as a thinker, often discussing with her the notoriously difficult work of Ludwig Wittgenstein.

20 Thomas Aquinas, *Selected Philosophical Writings*, sel. and trans. Timothy McDermott (New York: Oxford University Press, 1993), 88, 192 (emphasis added).

is "stuck" with people who neither love nor understand her. "Love and understanding are one and the same only in God," O'Connor replies. "Who do you think you understand? If anybody, you delude yourself. I love a lot of people, understand none of them. This is not perfect love but [it is] as much as a finite creature can be capable of. It all comes under the larger heading of what individuals have to suffer for the common good," O'Connor concludes, "[it's] a mystery, and part of the suffering of Christ" (HB, 543).

O'Connor also illumined the mystery of Hester's suffering in commenting on the short life and early death of Mary Ann, a young girl who had been grotesquely consumed by cancer[21] and who had been cared for by a congregation of Dominican nuns at Our Lady of Perpetual Help Home in Atlanta. "[Mary Ann] was equipped by natural intelligence and by a suitable education, not simply to endure [her suffering], but to build upon it. She was an extraordinarily rich little girl" (CW, 828). Mary Ann's wretchedly disfigured visage thus became the occasion for her participation in Christ's suffering, enabling her body to take its true form in a graciously embraced death.

Such a thoroughly embodied and sacramental participation in the suffering of Christ is the suffering that Betty Hester was finally unable to embrace. She abandoned the basic premise on which everything stands—the conviction, namely, that the cosmos is not an unsponsored and undirected process, but a magnificent gift-universe mysteriously ordered to the love and truth and beauty of God. She fled from it into the discarnate and anti-sacramental philosophy of Iris Murdoch. Rather than discerning her soul as the form of her body, she envisioned even her bodily self-destruction as the inevitable outgrowth of her unalterable spiritual self.

The Suicide of Elizabeth Hester

Thirty-six years after the death of Flannery O'Connor, Elizabeth Hester fired the lethal shot, on December 27, 1998. It was an immensely sad event, even as it was also a deeply anti-sacramental act. Hester was finally unable or unwilling to offer her suffering as the personal locus of the divine sacrifice. In an uncannily prescient letter from 1958, O'Connor wrote to Hester about a man who had killed himself: "His tragedy was I suppose that he

[21] She suffered from a neuroblastoma that pushed an eyeball out of its socket and onto her cheek.

didn't know what to do with his suffering" (HB, 287). It is not maudlin to suggest that the same holds true of Betty Hester: She did not know what to do with her suffering. In a similar letter, Flannery dealt with the suicide of the poet Hart Crane. She pointed out that, "though the act [of self-slaughter] may not have been good, good did come out of [it] . . . The Communion of Saints has something to do with the fact that the burdens we bear because *of* someone else, we can also bear *for* someone else" (HB, 178, emphasis added).

This last clause provides a telling summary of the eleven-year friendship of Elizabeth Hester and Flannery O'Connor. Burdened *by* each other's suffering, they were at least partly able to bear it *for* one another. In one of her final letters, Flannery goes out of her way to confess her own proclivity for fault-finding, while praising Betty for perceiving the worth of their mutual friend Bill Sessions: "your great natural grace is finding the good in people. It's a real gift. I never been bothered with it myself" (HB, 587).

It is important to remember that, while the Church has declared many souls to be definitively saved—they constitute what Scripture calls the "great cloud of witnesses" (Heb 12:1–2) and what the Church calls "the communion of saints"—it has never pronounced a single soul to be definitively damned, not even Judas. Whether human bodies have been sacramentally ensouled and thus redeemed is a judgment that only God can eternally decide. Yet proximate assessments remain necessary. O'Connor's remarkable response to Hester's first confession of her lesbianism is a profound instance of such discernment. She remarked that Job's alleged friends are the ones who are damned—not the suffering and doubting, the impatient and furiously protesting Job himself: "Compared to what you have experienced in the way of radical misery, I have never had anything to bear in my life but minor irritations, but there are times when the sharpest suffering is not to suffer and the worst affliction is not to be afflicted. Job's comforters were worse off than he was though they didn't know it."[22]

If "the sharpest suffering is not to suffer," then the keenest faith is to join one's own afflictions to the broken body of Christ. Betty Hester was finally unable or unwilling thus to offer her suffering to God. Yet neither was she afflicted in the dreadful and damning way of Job's false comforters; i.e., by remaining immune to affliction. Instead, she confessed it to her friend, in eleven years of remarkable correspondence. Hence our immense gratitude

22 October 31, 1956, unpublished letter.

to Elizabeth Hester, not of course for her self-immolation, but surely for enabling Flannery O'Connor to gain a fuller understanding, indeed to make a fuller embrace, of true friendship through sacramental suffering.

Such sacramental suffering is rooted and sustained by dogma, as Flannery O'Connor learned in no small part from St. John Henry Newman. To their relation, we now turn.

8

Living and Dying Upon Dogma

The Dogmatic Witness of Flannery O'Connor and John Henry Newman to a Post-Christian Culture

Introduction

It is difficult to imagine two more antithetical figures than John Henry Newman and Mary Flannery O'Connor. Newman the serene Christian humanist was also the consummate gentleman—the kind whom he famously described as "one who never inflicts pain."[1] O'Connor the slashing Christian satirist was a self-described hillbilly Thomist who inflicted satiric pain on all and sundry. If Evelyn Waugh doubted that *Wise Blood* could be "the unaided work of a young lady" (CW, 897), how much more would Saint John Henry have recoiled from fiction that includes a clubfooted delinquent who lies and steals because he says he's good at it (*The Lame Shall Enter First*); a little rich boy who drowns himself in search of the salvation his suave parents hold in contempt ("The River"); a baptizing backwoods prophet who deafened his own nephew by means of a Petrine blast with a shotgun (*The Violent Bear It Away*); a mass-murdering Misfit who, using a pistol as his catechetical tool, awakens a ladylike grandmother from her Christian apostasy, all the while complaining that Jesus has "thown" everything off balance ("A Good Man Is Hard to Find"); as well as a self-satisfied farmwife who thanks Jesus nightly for making her both white and prosperous—until she is slugged in the head with a social-science textbook hurled by a Wellesley student who calls her a warthog from Hell ("Revelation"). Rather than avoiding pain, O'Connor's unladylike fiction inflicts it on all sorts and conditions of her characters and readers.

Even allowing for their almost totally different circumstances, what did these seeming incommensurate figures have in common—the most

[1] John Henry Newman, *The Idea of a University*, ed. Martin J. Svaglic (Notre Dame, Ind.: University of Notre Dame Press, 1982 [1873]), 158.

famous nineteenth-century British Catholic convert on the one hand, and the most important twentieth-century American Catholic writer on the other?[2] The answer lies, I believe, in their mutual commitment to dogma. For both of them, dogma is central not only for the Church's own faith and practice, but also for Christian witness to a post-Christian culture sliding rapidly toward nihilism.

The Nature of Dogma

Few antidotes to the Age of Ashes and the Culture of Death would seem more counterintuitive than dogma. It is a word that makes many people scowl. It has almost entirely negative associations. Only the oppressive and intolerant are said to love dogma, and they are allegedly eager to push it down the throats of others. The Enlightenment developed such anti-dogmatic mottoes as "Deeds, not creeds" and "Dogmas divide, ethics unite." Immanuel Kant set dogma in its appropriately servile place as the lowly handmaiden to ethics: "The only thing that matters in religion is deeds. . . . Dogma is now . . . what we find . . . possible and useful for practical (moral) purposes. . . ."[3] Mark Twain states Kant's patronizing of dogma far more forcefully when, in *Pudd'nhead Wilson*, a schoolboy declares that "faith [i.e., dogma] is believing what you know ain't so."

Flannery O'Connor confessed, by contrast, that "My stories have been watered and fed by Dogma" (CW, 930). As compressed narrative distillations of God's self-identification in Israel and Christ and the Church, the creeds are "instrument[s] of freedom and not of restriction," as O'Connor insisted (CW, 943). "Christian dogma," she added, "is about the only thing left in the world that surely guards and respects mystery" (MM, 178). By "mystery" O'Connor does not refer to things that balk the mind and stifle understanding, but rather to the ultimate mystery of the Trinity itself. This *mysterion* alone can prompt both ever greater discovery and ever greater

2 O'Connor did not deny that Newman was somewhat fussy and fastidious. As she confessed to Elizabeth Hester in a letter from 1959, "If Newman is a saint, his saintliness didn't destroy his scrupulous intellect or his finickiness. . . . Anyway, he is here [in *Apologia Pro Vita Sua*] dealing with [Charles] Kingsley, enough to bring out the finickiness in anybody" (HB, 352).

3 Immanuel Kant, *The Conflict of the Faculties*, first part: "The conflict of the philosophy faculty with the theological faculty," in *Religion and Rational Theology*, trans. and ed. Allen W. Wood and George Di Giovanni (Cambridge: Cambridge University Press, 2009), 367.

ignorance. The greater one plumbs its depths, the greater grows one's need for further understanding.

Henri de Lubac helpfully defines *dogma* as the Church's "constituted thinking."[4] By this he means that, in its various councils and creeds, the Church has worked out those doctrinal claims which, because they are based on God's incarnational self-identification, are binding on all believers. In contrast to dogma, de Lubac defines *tradition* as the Church's "constitutive thinking."[5] By this he means that, in the Church's ongoing work of interpreting and expounding the Word of God for each succeeding age, it constantly though carefully elaborates its dogmas. Tradition ensures that dogmas do not become fixed and static. Therein lies their evolutionary enlargement. As Newman was among the first to emphasize, Christian doctrine remains true to itself by organically developing.[6] The original *depositum fidei*—the acorn of Christian revelation—continues to ramify into the great oak of Christian doctrine: What is originally embryonic thus undergoes constant maturation. The Church's magisterial tradition excavates this deposit of faith, endlessly mining its riches in order that the gold of the Gospel might shine ever more brightly.[7]

Dogmas are not statements about empirically verifiable facts made in the manner of customary claims about objects. Nor are they purely theoretical truths that can be divorced from their liturgical setting. On the contrary, dogmas serve a virtually sacramental function. They *convey* grace. They *enable* believers to encounter the reality of God's incomparably

[4] Henri de Lubac, *Catholicism: Christ and the Common Destiny of Man*, trans. Lancelot C. Sheppard and Sister Elizabeth Englund, OCD (San Francisco: Ignatius Press, 1988), 18.

[5] De Lubac, *Catholicism*, 18. In the literal chronological sense, dogma takes precedence even over scripture, since apostolic tradition was the means whereby the Church determined, out of the many early Christian texts, those biblical books which it regarded as canonical.

[6] One of Newman's most lasting achievements lies in his arguments concerning the evolutionary enlargement of dogma. He began this journey of discovery while still an Anglican, especially in his sermons preached at St. Mary's, Oxford; but it came to its grand climacteric in the final edition of *The Development of Dogma*.

[7] The dogmas of Trinity and Incarnation, for instance, are nowhere made explicit in the New Testament; yet the Church developed and defined these doctrines as necessary implications of scriptural claims about the divine nature and its earthly self-disclosure. Even the Marian dogmas, those doctrines that seem furthest removed from biblical attestation, are the theological outworkings of tradition. The Immaculate Conception (1854) and the Bodily Assumption (1950) are the two most obvious modern extensions of ancient dogmas concerning the Theotokos.

generous self-gift to the world. Creedal language, as Avery Dulles observes (while also citing Hans Urs von Balthasar), conveys "a truth greater and more serious than ordinary language is able to bear. Thus dogmatic speech, while it is irreducible to scientific or descriptive language, is by no means equivalent to mere subjective fantasy. The propositions of dogma 'are true insofar as they are a function and expression of the Church's understanding of the Christ-mystery, as given [to the Church] by the Holy Spirit.'"[8] The loss of such a sacramental regard for dogma, I will argue, has had devastating moral and religious consequences for our churches and our culture alike. The recently canonized John Henry Newman prophesied this calamity in his letters denouncing Sir Robert Peel's 1841 proposal to establish a religion-free reading room in his residential city.

Newman's Critique of Peel's Utilitarianism

Sir Robert Peel was the Member of Parliament for Tamworth, in Staffordshire east of Birmingham, from 1830 to 1850, having been made Prime Minister in 1834 by King William IV, the same year that Peel had founded what would become the modern Conservative party by way of the principles he laid out in his Tamworth Manifesto. Seven years later, upon his return as Prime Minister in 1841, Peel presided over the opening of a public reading room in his native city. Its library and lectures would be designed to lift artisans and members of the working classes out of their bondage to unscientific ways of supporting themselves and their families. At first glance, this seems a benign project. What, one must ask, could be dubious about Sir Robert's desire to distribute the latest pamphlets on "thorough draining and deep ploughing," on preventing diseases in wheat, on learning to create an annual balance sheet between gains and losses, even on finding means for emigration due to excessive competition that reduced capital profits?[9] Great agricultural and economic advances were being achieved through scientific experiment and testing, Peel boasted, heralding the new gospel of progress. Huge breakthroughs, especially in travel and communication, were creating a practical revolution by effacing "the interval between the producer and the consumer." To be uninformed

[8] Avery Robert Dulles, *The Survival of Dogma* (Garden City, N.Y.: Doubleday, 1971), 158.

[9] Sir Robert Peel, "The Opening of the Tamworth Library and Reading Room" (http://www.historyhome.co.uk/peel/education/tamread.htm).

about these technical discoveries and improvements was to be left hopelessly laggard in the task of getting financially ahead.

As an instinctive though largely apolitical fellow Conservative, Newman might have been expected to support Peel's program. Instead, he subjects its various proposals to acerbic scorn.[10] Among many other risible qualities in the Tamworth Address, Newman treats its naive Utilitarianism with scathing contempt. He rightly identifies what is sinister about the notions that knowledge has now become the means (and these are Peel's own words) of "taking care of number one—a clear appreciation of what is pleasurable, what painful, and what promotes the one and prevents the other. An uneducated man," according to Peel-cum-Bentham, "is ever mistaking his own interest, and standing in the way of his own true enjoyments. Useful Knowledge is that which tends to make us more useful to ourselves."[11] In becoming allegedly more useful to ourselves, Newman replies, we will also become more self-serving. An obsession with "getting and spending," as Wordsworth had already named it, will be the dread result. The rapid descent to a culture of comfort, convenience, and entertainment will soon follow. Wittily resorting to the Utilitarian reliance on economic metaphors, Newman prophesies that Peel and his sort "will find themselves outbid in the market by gratifications much closer at hand, and on a level with the meanest capacity."[12]

The World as a Machine or as the Work of God?

As the evangel for this brave new world of omnicompetent science and technics, Sir Robert trumpets the good news that we humans are distinguished "from the Beasts that perish" by our capacity for "indefinite

[10] That Newman was unwilling either to conflate the Gospel with political conservatism or to make it the basis for an attack on political liberalism is noteworthy: He is no culture-warrior *avant la lettre*. Indeed, Newman includes his own Conservatives in naming the various surrogates that are often substituted for authentic Faith—the false faith that becomes merely the instrumental means for achieving political ends: "What *is* Christianity? Universal benevolence? Exalted morality? Supremacy of law? Conservatism? An age of light? An age of reason? Which of them all?" (John Henry Newman, *Discussions and Arguments on Various Subjects* [London: Longmans, Green, 1891], 278.)

[11] Newman, *Discussions and Arguments*, 262. "The Tamworth Reading Room Letters," included in this volume, were first published in 1841.

[12] Newman, *Discussions and Arguments*, 267.

enquiry."[13] Peel seems oblivious to the implications of his adjective. "Indefinite" literally means without regard to any well-defined *finis* or end. Hence the real gravamen of Peel's claim is that the burgeoning exploration of nature's operations should be conducted apart from any transcendent aim or limit for such research. The echoes of Kant's generalized summons to all and sundry—*Sapere aude!*—are unmistakable.

Little did Peel recognize that there is a long tradition opposed to Kant's supposedly daring call to know for the sake of knowing. Even Newman himself fails to note Augustine's caution against *curiositas* in the *Confessions*. There Augustine warns against the unguided desire to seek out things that may yield one knows not what. In similar fashion, Dante places the Greek hero Ulysses deep within the circles of his *Inferno*. Far from being a heroic figure because he sailed through the Straits of Gibraltar into the uncharted Atlantic, Ulysses damnably risked the lives of his men and the eternal destiny of his own soul in seeking such untethered discovery. No wonder that Ulysses and his men drown when they crash on Mount Purgatory, the huge seven-storey promontory that rises up out of the southern seas, for they lacked the one thing requisite for ascending the Holy Mountain: humility. So it is with Milton, who dares to speak of "forbidden knowledge" in *Paradise Lost*—i.e., a knowledge of things which fallen humanity is unprepared to master with skill and proficiency without dreadful results. Nor should we forget that Milton wrote his great poem in the same century that Descartes was boasting of his desire to become a "master and possessor of nature."

Even though Newman offers no such caveats against Peel, he vigorously challenges Peel's naïve way of interpreting the natural order as a neutral realm whose mastery will have only salutary physical effects without any deleterious moral and spiritual effects. Hence Newman's clear distinction between two ways of viewing the world, carefully employing the adverb "as" to remind his readers that all seeing is "seeing as": "There are two ways, then, of reading Nature—*as* a machine and *as* a work. If we come to it with the assumption that it is a creation, we shall study it with awe; if assuming it to be a system, with mere curiosity."[14] Assumptions and predispositions, it follows, are all-determining. To deny them is to wear Enlightenment blinkers unawares. It is to assume that there is a

13 Peel, "Opening of the Tamworth Library and Reading Room."

14 Newman, *Discussions and Arguments*, 300 (emphasis added). I owe this insight to Barry Harvey.

value-neutral, eagle-eyrie "view from nowhere," a supposedly impartial "curiosity" that has no religious or ethical consequence.

Physicalism and Its Terrors

Such allegedly lensless seeing is in fact already lensed with Newtonian spectacles. It can discern the world only as an unbroken chain of efficient causes and their inexorable effects. Like William Blake, Newman was among the first to insist that the result is a barren physicalism.[15] "Physical philosophers," Newman observes, "are ever inquiring *whence* things are, not *why*, referring them to [visible] nature, not to [invisible] mind; and thus they tend to make a [physical] system a substitute for a God." Once reason is untethered from its divine *telos*, Newman concludes, it beholds the operations of nature as would William Paley or James Watts—i.e., as akin to "a watch or a steam-carriage."[16]

Far from denying the truth of bare-naked physicalism, Newman affirms it as frightfully as does Darwin or any of his latter-day epigoni:

> Our first feeling [upon moving from the divine to the natural and human sphere] is one of surprise and (I may say) of dismay, that His control of this living world is so indirect, His action so obscure. . . . What strikes the mind so forcibly and so painfully is, His absence (if I may so speak) from His own world. It is a silence that speaks. It is as if others had got possession of His work. Why does not He, our Maker and Ruler, give us some immediate knowledge of Himself? Why does He not write His Moral Nature in large letters upon the face of history, and bring the blind, tumultuous rush of events into

15 Physicalism, according to Alisdair MacIntyre, remains a more accurate term than either naturalism or materialism. This is especially true for Christians, since nature and matter are indispensable categories for those who believe that God is the creator and sustainer of Nature, and that, in assuming Matter in the Christ, he has redeemed the fallen material world no less than its sinful spiritual counterpart.

16 Newman, *Discussions and Arguments*, 299–300. Earlier in the "Tamworth Reading Room Letters," he had made the point that there is no reasoning without axioms and presuppositions: "Life is not long enough for a religion of inferences; we shall never have done beginning, if we determine to begin with proof. We shall ever be laying our foundations; we shall turn theology into evidences, and divines into textuaries. We shall never get at our first principles. Resolve to believe nothing, and you must prove your proofs and analyze your elements, sinking further and further, and finding 'in the lowest depth a lower deep,' till you come to the broad bosom of scepticism" (295).

> a celestial, hierarchical order? . . . I see only a choice of alternative explanations of so critical a fact:—either there is no Creator, or He has disowned His creatures.[17]

Unlike eighteenth-century deists, but also unlike recent advocates of so-called "intelligent design," Newman insists that no Christian understanding of God can be derived from such a physicalist conception: "What the physical creation presents to us *in itself* is a piece of machinery, and when men speak of a Divine Intelligence as its Author, this god of theirs is not the Living and True, unless the spring is the god of a watch, or steam the creator of the engine."[18] Hence Newman's insistence on what all physicalists, from Francis Bacon to Francis Crick, fail to acknowledge. He states it in the final and peremptory sentence of his last Tamworth letter: "a body without a soul has no life."[19] The universe, understood apart from the dogmas of Creation and Redemption, appears to be a massive mechanism, a gargantuan cosmic body without a life-giving soul.

Works of Controversial Divinity Shall Not Be Admitted

Matthew Arnold and other humanists might have joined Newman's attack on Peel's brittle utilitarianism and physicalism. What made Newman recoil in wrath—as it would not have stung Arnold—was this single brazen claim: "The first fundamental rule" of the Tamworth Reading Room Society, Sir Robert declared, is "that works of Controversial Divinity shall not be admitted into the Library," and that lectures held there would

[17] John Henry Newman, *An Essay in Aid of a Grammar of Assent* (Garden City, N.Y.: Doubleday Image, 1955), 309. Newman concedes that "the *accidental* evolution of organic beings" does not negate divine design. What Darwin failed to discern is that natural selection is "accidental to *us*, not to God" (quoted in John Cornwell, *Newman's Unquiet Grave: The Reluctant Saint* [London: Continuum, 2011], 236). Newman is no less glum about the course of human events:

> . . . the defeat of good, the success of evil, physical pain, mental anguish, the prevalence and intensity of sin, the pervading idolatries, the corruptions, the dreary hopeless irreligion, that condition of the whole race, so fearfully yet exactly described in the Apostle's words, "having no hope and without God in the world", all this is to dizzy and appal; and inflicts upon the mind the sense of profound mystery, which is absolutely above human solution. (Quoted in Cornwell, *Newman's Unquiet Grave*, 165)

[18] Newman, *Discussions and Arguments*, 302 (emphasis added).

[19] Newman, *Discussions and Arguments*, 302.

exclude "everything calculated to excite religious animosities."[20] Like the Hobbes whom he would have abhorred, Peel feared that religion is likely to become unruly, indeed subversive to state order, unless it is subjected to governmental control. Since Christian dogma spawns public controversy and perhaps political unrest, it should be confined to the ecclesial realm.

With remarkable prescience, Newman names what is most truly pernicious about Peel's seemingly forward-looking proposal. Its prohibition against theological texts and ideas from such a public-sponsored reading room was, in fact, a means of exiling dogma to the private and virtually invisible realm of mere opinion. Already in his Tamworth Letters of 1841, the still-Anglican Newman was prophesying against the evil that he would identify most memorably in his "Biglietto Speech" almost forty years later upon being elevated to the cardinalate in 1879—namely, that his whole life had been a struggle against *liberalism.*

Philosophical Liberalism as the Triumph of Private Judgment

Lest this seem to make Newman an arch-reactionary, it must be remembered that he defines liberalism in religious rather than political terms: It is "the anti-dogmatic principle." By this he means that subjective judgment has trumped all other considerations: "There is no existing authority on earth competent to interfere with the liberty of individuals in reasoning and judging for themselves. . . . There are rights of conscience such, that every one may lawfully advance a claim to profess and teach what is false and wrong in matters, religious, social, and moral, provided that to his private conscience it seems absolutely true and right."[21] This liberal appeal to the rule of private judgment, now completely dissevered from all transcendent norms, leads to the worst of all outcomes—the endless proliferation of individual opinions as incontestable truths.

Newman does not deny the contingent character of knowledge. He in fact anticipates Wittgenstein, Toulmin, MacIntyre, and many others in acknowledging that all truth is lensed, that we are all wearing spectacles, that all knowledge is historical all the way down. He is not convinced, however, that all religious truths are equal. He insists, instead, that Christians adjudicate among them by recourse to revealed dogmas as they have been historically mediated through the Church. Liberalism, by contrast,

[20] Newman, *Discussions and Arguments*, 302.

[21] John Henry Newman, *Apologia Pro Vita Sua*, ed. David J. DeLaura (New York: W.W. Norton Critical Edition, 1968), 223.

embraces an absolute liberty of thought that lands itself in an incorrigible relativism that cannot correct its mistakes:

> Whenever men are able to act at all, there is the chance of extreme and intemperate action; and therefore, when there is exercise of mind, there is the chance of wayward or mistaken exercise. Liberty of thought is in itself a good; but it gives an opening to false liberty. Now by Liberalism I mean false liberty of thought, or the exercise of thought upon matters, in which, from the constitution of the human mind, thought cannot be brought to any successful issue, and therefore is out of place. Among such matters are first principles of whatever kind; and of these the most sacred and momentous are especially to be reckoned the truths of Revelation. Liberalism then is the mistake of subjecting to human judgment those revealed doctrines which are in their nature beyond and independent of it, and of claiming to determine on intrinsic grounds the truth and value of propositions which rest for their reception simply on the external authority of the Divine Word.[22]

[22] Newman, *Discussions and Arguments*, 218. For Newman—as also for the more recent advocates of the *nouvelle théologie*—revelation precedes and enables reason, so that there is no such thing as pure reason or ungraced nature:

> Where Revealed Truth has given the aim and direction to Knowledge, Knowledge of all kinds will minister to Revealed Truth. The evidences of Religion, natural theology, metaphysics,—or, again, poetry, history, and the classics,—or physics and mathematics, may all be grafted into the mind of a Christian, and give and take by the grafting. *But if in education we begin with nature before grace, with evidences before faith, with science before conscience, with poetry before practice, we shall be doing much the same as if we were to indulge the appetites and passions, and turn a deaf ear to the reason.* In each case we misplace what in its place is a divine gift. If we attempt to effect a moral improvement by means of poetry, we shall but mature into a mawkish, frivolous, and fastidious sentimentalism;—if by means of argument, into a dry, unamiable long-headedness;—if by good society, into a polished outside, with hollowness within, in which vice has lost its grossness, and perhaps increased its malignity;—if by experimental science, into an uppish, supercilious temper, much inclined to scepticism. But reverse the order of things: put Faith first and Knowledge second; let the University minister to the Church, and then classical poetry becomes the type of Gospel truth, and physical science a comment on Genesis or Job, and Aristotle changes into Butler, and Arcesilas into Berkeley. (274–75, emphasis added)

Dogmas Practiced in the Christian Life

These "revealed doctrines" are not to be affirmed via a mindless fideism, a *sacrificium intellectum*. They are matters of faith whose evidence lies chiefly in the living of them. As Newman would later argue in *The Grammar of Assent*, virtually all of our basic assumptions lie beyond any demonstration, much less any independent formulation of them, either by or for ourselves. They are accessible only by what he calls "the illative sense," his term for what Aristotle named as *phronesis* or prudence. We act according to assumptions that we cannot prove except in their practice.

In accord with Scripture, Newman insists that belief is first a matter of the heart more than the mind, of obedience more than knowledge. Christian faith, for him, is a matter of lifelong conversion of conscience, a gradual reconstitution of body and soul alike, a slow and total transformation of human existence through a process that the ancient Church called *theosis* or deification. In *The Idea of a University*, Newman reveals his own prescription for such a life, whether it be intellectual or religious: "I should not rely on sudden, startling effects, but on the slow, silent, penetrating, overpowering effects of patience, steadiness, routine, and perseverance."[23] In his novel *Loss and Gain*, one of Newman's characters vividly describes the kind of person whom a rightly-formed conscience is meant to produce: "A man's moral self is concentrated in each moment of his life; it lives in the tips of his fingers, and the springs of his insteps."

Such *real*, as over against mere "notional," assent to the triune God entails no sudden leap of faith or lonely act of will. It is a consequence, writes John Cornwell, "of encountering the Christian religion, its people, its objects, and its practices over time. . . . [It] involves imaginative apprehensions of its prayers and sacraments, its rituals and Scriptures, its Creed, and all the tangible, visual and concrete expressions of Christian faith. Above all it involves the presence of Jesus Christ in our imaginations, in the Eucharist, and in the community of the Church."[24]

Freedom Ordered to the Good Given by God

With remarkable prescience, Newman discerns what happens when we abandon such imaginative apprehension of the Church's creeds and the prophetic embodiments of its practices. On one hand, moral liberty will

[23] John Henry Cardinal Newman, *The Idea of a University: Defined and Illustrated* (London: Longmans, Green, and Co., 1889), 493.

[24] Cornwell, *Newman's Unquiet Grave*, 184.

be defined negatively in accord with John Stuart Mill as doing no physical harm to others. On the other hand, it will be construed positively in accord with late-modern democratic theory as constructing one's own life without let or hindrance. The individualist results, alas, are much the same. Liberty untethered from religious dogma produces the delusion that, as if we were gods, we can create ourselves *ex nihilo*, making up our identity according to our own sweet desires.

Newman contends, exactly to the contrary, that only when freedom is ordered to the Good—when liberty is understood as obedience directed toward the *finis* or *telos* given by God—can we be delivered from bondage to self-interest. Hence the rhetorical climax of Newman's denunciation of Sir Robert Peel's project:

> The heart is commonly reached, not through the reason, but through the imagination, by means of direct impressions, by the testimony of facts and events, by history, by description. Persons influence us, voices melt us, looks subdue us, deeds inflame us. *Many a man will live and die upon a dogma: no man will be a martyr for a conclusion.* . . . This is why a literary religion is so little to be depended upon; it looks well in fair weather, but its doctrines are opinions, and, when called to suffer for them, [such literary faith] slips [its opinions] between its folios, or burns them at its hearth.[25]

By history and facts and events, by persons and deeds and dogmas, Newman does not assume that there is any allegedly neutral calculus for measuring them; he refers, instead, to the Church's two-millennial witness to them. In this remarkable statement, Newman is calling for the

[25] Newman, *Discussions and Arguments*, 293 (emphasis added). Flannery O'Connor heavily underlined and marked the margins of her own copy of *A Grammar of Assent*, this passage that Newman had retained from his earlier attack on Peel (Arthur F. Kinney, *Flannery O'Connor's Library: Resources of Being* [Athens: University of Georgia Press, 1985], 45). O'Connor is also likely to have affirmed the beginning of this same paragraph: "Science gives us the grounds or premisses from which religious truths are to be inferred; but it does not set about inferring them, much less does it reach the inference;—that is not its province. It brings before us phenomena, and it leaves us, if we will, to call them works of design, wisdom, or benevolence; and further still, if we will, to proceed to confess an Intelligent Creator. We have to take its facts, and to give them a meaning, and to draw our own conclusions from them. First comes Knowledge, then a view, then reasoning, and then belief. This is why Science has so little of a religious tendency; deductions have no power of persuasion" (*Discussions and Arguments*, 293).

Church—rather than civic-minded savants represented by Peel—to serve as the prime locus of human transformation. Hence its urgently needed service to a moribund world. Victory over the twin giants that Newman called "the passion and the pride of man" comes neither by scientific endeavor nor humanistic learning so long as these deny their limited character. Noble as such endeavors often are, they may produce monstrosity no less than humanity. Newman acknowledges that the Church has produced her own monsters, of course, but always and only in violation of her own sacraments and teachings. For Newman, the stony heart of humanity can be turned into what the prophet Ezekiel calls "a heart of flesh" (36:26–27) only by radical obedience to the commands of the crucified and risen Lord as he is witnessed in the revealed dogmas and sacraments, in the unique teachings and practices of the Church, in the lives and deaths of ordinary believers no less than the saints.[26]

The Church, insofar as it views things through the aperture of God's historically mediated revelation in Israel and Christ, can envision the world

[26] Newman is a thorough-going Aristotelian in his conviction that the moral life is primarily a matter of habits and practices acquired largely through the example and imitation of masters, rather than through reading and thinking alone:

> Knowledge is one thing, virtue is another; good sense is not conscience, refinement is not humility, nor is largeness and justness of view faith. Philosophy, however enlightened, however profound, gives no command over the passions, no influential motives, no vivifying principles. Liberal Education makes not the Christian, not the Catholic, but the gentleman. It is well to be a gentlemen, it is well to have a cultivated intellect, a delicate taste, a candid, equitable, dispassionate mind, a noble and courteous bearing in the conduct of life;—these are the connatural qualities of a large knowledge; they are the objects of a University; I am advocating, I shall illustrate and insist upon them; but still, I repeat, they are no guarantee for sanctity or even for conscientiousness, they may attach to the man of the world, to the profligate, to the heartless,—pleasant, alas, and attractive as he shows when decked out in them. Taken by themselves, they do but seem to be what they are not; they look like virtue at a distance, but they are detected by close observers, and on the long run; and hence it is that they are popularly accused of pretence and hypocrisy, not, I repeat, from their own fault, but because their professors and their admirers persist in taking them for what they are not, and are officious in arrogating for them a praise to which they have no claim. *Quarry the granite rock with razors, or moor the vessel with a thread of silk; then may you hope with such keen and delicate instruments as human knowledge and human reason to contend against those giants, the passion and the pride of man.* (Newman, *Idea of a University*, 91, emphasis added)

as a moral work rather than as an amoral machine. And because Creation is inseparably joined to Redemption, the Church also has the capacity to make truly moral men and women, those who are able to repent and be transformed into the image of Christ.[27] Hence Newman's conclusion that the Church makes its most decisive witness to its post-Christian culture by an unabashed dedication to dogmas worth living and dying for.

Flannery O'Connor on Dogma as the Final Guarantor of Mystery

The animating core of O'Connor's work is made evident, as we have heard, in her celebrated confession that her stories are "watered and fed by Dogma" (CW, 930), and that, if she did not see through the lenses of dogma, she would see nothing at all. "Dogma is an instrument for penetrating reality," O'Connor insists. "Christian dogma is about the only thing left in the world that surely guards and respects mystery" (MM, 178). O'Connor's critics sometimes complain that, in making such confessions, she was attempting to control, even to manipulate, the interpretation of her fiction, not only during her short life but also from the grave. O'Connor's work must be construed in a dogmatic Catholic fashion, such critics complain, or else they are allegedly misconstrued.

These dissenters fail to discern that O'Connor's well-wrought fiction, like the Church's carefully developed dogmas, embodies a mystery that *cannot* be mastered. The Greek word *mysterion* does not mean mystification. It is not a bewilderment of the mind that silences speech and balks reason. "To St. Paul and to the early Christian thinkers," writes O'Connor's favorite Old Testament scholar Claude Tresmontant, mystery is "the particular object of intelligence, its fullest nourishment. The *mysterion* is something so rich in intelligible content, so inexhaustibly full of delectation for the mind that no contemplation can ever reach its end. [Mystery] is an eternal delectation of the mind."[28] St. Paul likens the *mysterion* of

27 Newman, *Discussions and Arguments*, 284.

28 Quoted in John Desmond, *Risen Sons: Flannery O'Connor's Vision of History* (Athens: University of Georgia Press, 1987), 9. The Orthodox bishop Kallistos Ware makes a similar claim:

> In the proper religious sense of the term, "mystery" signifies not only hiddenness but disclosure. The Greek noun *mysterion* [which can also be translated "sacrament"] is linked with the verb *myein*, meaning "to close the eyes or mouth." The candidate for initiation into certain of the pagan mystery religions was first blindfolded and led through a maze of passages; then

living in the power of Christ's death and resurrection to the planting and sprouting of a seed (1 Cor 15:51), as does the Fourth Gospel (John 12:24).

Almost a half century after her death, her stories and novels continue to have an endlessly fructifying effect because they are rooted, not in human-all-too-human claims, but in suprahuman dogmatic claims. Whether ancient or modern, dogmas lie beyond human manipulation, whenever they do their proper work either in faith or fiction. The unknowable God who eludes all human categories—even the negative descriptions of divinity found in apophatic theology—this unknowable God is revealed in mysteries that not only preserve the unfathomable quality of the divine nature itself but also invite unending participation in God's own triune life.

More than any other reader of O'Connor, John Sykes rebuts the charge that O'Connor is an oppressively dogmatic and thus a monologic author. He rightly insists that O'Connor surpasses the limits of the monologic word by becoming a dialogic writer "in an apophatic sense: for her, the highest use of language was to prepare us to encounter something beyond language. . . . When O'Connor wrote, she was hoping that her stories would become the words of institution [in the Eucharist] that transform the stuff of earthly life into the body of God. . . . Thus might we say that for O'Connor the ultimate aim of fiction is not dialogue, but communion."[29]

Flannery O'Connor on Sight and Vision

O'Connor makes much the same distinction as Newman's two ways of "seeing as" when she describes a literary prophet as a realist of distances, one who is able to see far things close at hand, often like the blind man

> suddenly his eyes were uncovered and he saw, displayed all round him, the secret emblems of the cult. So, in the Christian context, we do not mean by a "mystery" merely that which is baffling and mysterious, an enigma or insoluble problem. A mystery is, on the contrary, something that is *revealed* for our understanding, but which we never understand *exhaustively* because it leads into the depth or the darkness of God. The eyes are closed—but they are also open.

Kallistos Ware, *The Orthodox Way* (Yonkers, N.Y.: St. Vladimir's Seminary Press, 1995), 15, emphasis original.

29 John D. Sykes Jr., *Flannery O'Connor, Walker Percy, and the Aesthetic of Revelation* (Columbia: University of Missouri Press, 2007), 78, 84.

whom Jesus cured and who then saw people as trees walking.[30] Here she is distinguishing between sight and vision. Sight is an *optical* act, a seeing by means of the *organ* of the eye, viewing things as with a telescope or a microscope, discerning their shapes and causes. Vision by contrast, is an *ocular* act, a beholding of things through the *mind* of the eye, the *oculus mentis* that penetrates depths and telescopes years, even centuries and millennia, by way of sacramental vision. Such vision is formed by dogmatic convictions about God and humanity and the world. Prophetic and sacramental vision discerns ultimate realities as being at once terribly near and transcendently distant, espying within the visible world what is not apparent, what is not obvious, but what is scandalously true, grotesquely good, even freakishly beautiful. This vision of the invisible requires a dogma-formed imagination in order to descry worldly analogues of both likeness and unlikeness to God. There is hardly a better justification of O'Connor's recourse to the strange and the odd, to the peculiar and the weird, to the mangled and mutilated, than a saying of Denys the Areopagite: "Similitudes drawn from things farthest away from God form within us a truer estimate that God is above whatsoever we may say or think of Him."[31]

The world that appears to be a merciless machine or a mindless clock when viewed with the eye of Enlightenment sight becomes, by contrast, the theater of God's own self-demonstration when discerned through the visionary eye of dogma. Far from taking leave of nature and history, dogma-shaped Christians discern both the natural and human worlds as saturated with divinity[32]—so that the Incarnation constitutes the cen-

[30] Vision "eventually involves the whole personality," she wrote, "and as much of the world as can be got into it" (MM, 91). Hence O'Connor's adoption of Joseph Conrad's motto as her own: "My task which I am trying to achieve is, by the power of the written word, to make you hear, to make you feel—it is, before all, is to make you *see*" (quoted in MM, 80).

[31] Quoted in Alison Milbank, *Chesterton and Tolkien as Theologians: The Fantasy of the Real* (New York: T&T Clark, 2007), 67.

[32] O'Connor attached a paper clip to p. 128 of Louis Bouyer's *Newman: His Life and His Spirituality* (New York: Meridian, 1960), perhaps because she was drawn to this particular passage: "It is no Platonic ideal world with which we are concerned, but with the eternal world which draws us on beyond this transitory world but which is nevertheless present in it, *embodied in every tree and hid behind every hill*. This is the very essence of the Christian faith. . . . And this invisible world is essentially a world of personal presences. And therefore it is by a linking of person with person that we come to it" (emphasis original).

tripetal, saving Core of human existence, while everything that centrifugally spins away from it becomes deadly. Hence O'Connor's wise counsel to Alfred Corn, an Emory University freshman (and future poet of considerable distinction), when he confessed that his collegiate studies had caused him to doubt his Christianity. O'Connor reminds him that doubt is intrinsic to faith, especially amidst our terror-and-death-drenched times, and thus that Corn should not dismiss his unbelief so much as to ask for greater faith. She also urges him not to let his intellectual life drown his imaginative life, especially as it can be energized by the sacramental mysteries of the Church. "Mystery isn't something that is gradually evaporating," she wrote to Corn. "It grows along with knowledge" (CW, 1174).[33]

Conclusion

Religiously no less than chronologically, Mary Flannery O'Connor lived and wrote at a much later time than John Henry Newman. Unlike him, she could not assume that America was an officially Christian nation with an established state Church, nor could she appeal to Christian leaders in Newman's fashion. Even less could she make a broad cultural appeal, through a series of public letters, for the Church to live and die upon dogma as the true alternative to a culture hurtling towards nihilism. It is much too late for Christians to save the West, as if ever this were the Church's chief mission. Yet O'Connor and Newman offer a powerful challenge to Christians of all sorts and conditions. They make it blindingly evident that, unless their faith and practice remain grounded and steeped in dogma, the Church will become ever more invisible, as Christians will enervate their encounter with the immortal Mystery that completes and perfects and transforms mortal truth.

Without this radical renovation of human sight into transcendent vision, Christians will also leave their Church and their culture stranded on Dover Beach. There, O'Connor and Newman both predict, we shall hear nothing other than the melancholy, long, withdrawing roar of the sea of Enlightenment unbelief, as the night wind of its arid physicalism sighs with an ever-retreating breath, and as the diminishing waves of its non- and often anti-Christian humanism finally wash out on the drear and naked shingles of nothingness. Dogmatically formed Christians, by contrast, will have the capacity to form small but faithful communities

[33] O'Connor also urged Corn to read Newman's *A Grammar of Assent* as well as Gilson's *The Unity of Philosophical Experience* (CW, 1165).

envisioned by Emeritus Pope Benedict XVI, seeking to offer radical witness to the sacramental and prophetic Gospel, exercising the privilege of living and dying upon dogma.

Dogmas do not dwell in airy isolation from everyday quandaries and vexations, least of all in sublime indifference to the chief scandal of American history—the injustices committed against African Americans. Flannery O'Connor confronts this scandal in many places, perhaps most tellingly in her treatment of her black characters. Finally, therefore, we must attend to them.

9

Flannery O'Connor's Black Characters

Race Revisited[1]

"I'm an integrationist by principle & a segregationist by taste. I don't *like* negroes. They all give me a pain & and the more of them I see, the less and less I like them. Particularly the new kind."[2] These sentences that will bring lasting infamy for Flannery O'Connor were penned on May 3, 1964, exactly three months before her death of lupus erythematosus at age thirty-nine. They were addressed to her friendly antagonist Maryat Lee, who often posed as the pluperfect Yankee liberal, even as O'Connor assumed her antic role as the unreconstructed Southern racist. It matters not. Any attempt to vindicate such statements would serve only to confirm the charges.

Once Angela Alaimo O'Donnell made this confession public in 2020, a veritable volcano of outrage erupted. Among other cancellations, perhaps the most notable was the chiseling of Flannery O'Connor's name from a Loyola University Baltimore dormitory where black women would be living. Having seen O'Connor's statement in O'Donnell's book, Paul Elie published a *New Yorker* essay with a willfully incendiary title: "How Racist

1 I have dealt at length with the race question in *Flannery O'Connor and the Christ-Haunted South* (Grand Rapids: Eerdmans, 2004), 93–119. See also Ralph C. Wood, "'Where Is the Voice Coming From?' Flannery O'Connor on Race," *Flannery O'Connor Bulletin* 22 (1993–1994): 90–118. Sally Fitzgerald's response, together with my reply, appeared in *Flannery O'Connor Bulletin* 23 (1994–1995): 175–83.

2 Quoted in Angela Alaimo O'Donnell, *Radical Ambivalence: Race in Flannery O'Connor* (New York: Fordham, 2020), 19. Further references will be paginated within the text as O.

Was Flannery O'Connor?" Rather than promising a trial by jury, Elie declared her guilty in advance.[3]

Although Angela O'Donnell led the losing fight against the canceling of Flannery O'Connor at the Loyola dormitory, she scores the writer for allegedly tranquilizing her conscience against the racial injustices being committed everywhere around her. O'Donnell's central contention is that O'Connor remained radically, indeed fatally, ambivalent about race. It must be admitted that O'Connor was ambivalent about the civil rights struggle, but for reasons that O'Donnell fails to fathom. O'Connor noted, for example, that northern protestors traveled southward by leaving behind cities that were rife with their own racial problems, coming "from afar with moral energy in direct proportion to their distance from home." For O'Connor there could be no convenient binary designating the South as evil and the North as good. "Good and evil," she wrote, "appear to be joined in every culture at the spine" (MM, 200). They take different forms in different regions. There is no calculus for measuring them.[4]

O'Donnell claims that O'Connor found "the efforts of civil rights activists to be a form of folly, at best, and a collective act of overweening pride, at worst. The puny efforts of human beings cannot bring about the victory of good over evil, and to witness people trying to achieve this constitutes both a sad and comic enterprise" (O, 80). This is a nonsense accusation in view of O'Donnell's own citation of O'Connor's counter-confession to Bill Sessions: "I feel very good about those changes in the South that have been

[3] Paul Elie, "How Racist Was Flannery O'Connor?" *New Yorker*, June 22, 2020. Elie seriously misreads the final scene of "Revelation" as confirming O'Connor's incurable racism: "Turpin's vision . . . is a segregationist's vision, in which people process to Heaven by race and class, equal but separate, white landowners such as Turpin preceded (the last shall be first) by 'bands of black niggers in white robes, and battalions of freaks and lunatics shouting and clapping and leaping like frogs.'" Elie is evidently unaware that Purgatory requires the moral and religious cleansing of those who remain *as yet* unfit for Paradise. Why are Ruby and Claud Turpin marching *last* in this dancing and singing and clapping purgatorial procession? It's not because they are bigots, as Elie thinks, but because they must *first* have their small-bore virtues—"good order and common sense and respectable behavior" (CW, 654)—burned away.

[4] O'Connor may have been ambivalent about the civil rights struggle, not only because she opposed its often-unexamined assumptions, but also because she feared that it bypassed the ultimate question: Even when—if ever?—the punishment of white civil wrongs and the restoration of black civil rights are accomplished, what is the eternal status of such sinners, black and white alike? Where, *coram Deo*, do they finally stand?

long overdue—the whole racial picture. I think it is improving by the minute, particularly in Georgia, and I don't see how anyone can feel otherwise than good about that" (O, 20).

O'Donnell partially compensates for her error by comparing Flannery O'Connor to Dorothy Day. In 1957, Day had traveled to Koinonia, Clarence Jordan's revolutionary venture in interracial Christian living, where blacks and whites operated a small self-sustaining farm near Americus, Georgia. While Day was visiting Koinonia, local white thugs harassed it with potentially deadly gunfire. O'Donnell praises Day for such political courage as compared to O'Connor's political quietism:

> Day is motivated by her faith as well as her political leanings, by the Church's contention that all human beings, black and white, are loved by God and equal in his eyes. Day, unlike O'Connor, is not "of two minds" about the race question or what actions one ought to take. O'Connor is clearly aware of this difference between herself and her fellow Catholic, begrudgingly admitting to Day's holiness—a holiness that would, eventually, put her on the path to canonization. She sees her own weakness here, admits her racial ambivalence, and expresses "hope" that her way of thinking and course of (in)action does not make her morally culpable. (O, 82)

O'Donnell is right to honor Day's courageous social witness. She was an ethical exemplar as O'Connor was not. Yet it is proper to ask whether these two eminent American Catholics were called, not (as O'Donnell maintains) to antithetical but rather to complementary vocations. Day made the Church visible via the Catholic Worker Movement, and she will long be esteemed for it. Yet the question of priority remains: Which of these two goods relies primarily on the other? It is obvious that there could have been a Dorothy Day without a Flannery O'Connor. Yet without the prior and eternal Word that prompted Day's mission, it would never have been born. O'Connor made drastic literary witness to that Word, and it shall last as long as human words shall last.

Jacques Maritain on the Irreducibility of Art to the Artist

Jacques Maritain, perhaps the most influential Catholic theologian of the twentieth century, provided Flannery O'Connor artistic liberty from biographical reductionism. From Maritain she learned that art is a virtue of the practical intellect. Art is "focused not on the mind as such but on action," as Rowan Williams explains, on "the right use of freedom for the human good." There is no guarantee, of course, that art will have such a salutary result. "Virtuous making aims," therefore, "not at the good of humanity but at the good of what is made." "What matters is what *this* work requires; a feature may be in itself jarring or even terrible, but may still be 'what pleases' in its context."[5] O'Connor offered her own concise summary of Maritain's influence:

> St. Thomas called art "reason in making." This is a very cold and very beautiful definition, and if it is unpopular today, this is because reason has lost ground among us. As grace and nature have been separated, so imagination and reason have been separated, and this always means an end to art. The artist uses his reason to discover an answering reason in everything he sees. For him, to be reasonable is to find, in the object, in the situation, in the sequence, the spirit which makes it itself. This is not an easy or simple thing to do. It is to intrude upon the timeless, and that is only done by the violence of a single-minded respect for the truth. (MM, 82–83)

This "beautifully cold" definition of art enabled O'Connor to devote herself doggedly to her craft, making it her "habit of being," as she achieved artistic proficiency by long and hard practice. Hence her confession that "Writing is a good example of self-abandonment. I never completely forget myself except when I am writing, and I am never more completely myself than when I am writing" (HB, 458). Despite her scorn for sanctimony, she experienced something akin to holiness during the two arduous hours spent every morning at the typewriter. The former Archbishop of Canterbury elucidates it:

> The artist exercises intellect with such detachment that the effect is a sort of image of sanctity, a contemplative absorption in what is truly there. And this needs to be said clearly, not to exalt the status of the artist to that of the saint, but precisely to counter any such idea, any 'messianism' about the artist's role, any slippage towards what the later Maritain calls the magical fallacy of which artists may be victims—that is, the notion that the artist's proper calling is to change the world according to his or her vision.[6]

[5] Rowan Williams, *Art and Necessity: Reflections on Art and Love* (Harrisburg, Pa.: Morehouse, 2005), 10, 11, 12.

[6] Williams, *Art and Necessity*, 16.

To put oneself into "the service of the thing [one] is making," is to be freed from the emotivist idea that fiction is a form of self-expression, as well as the moralist idea that art must edify its audience. The true aim of fiction is to contain nothing extraneous and subartistic, but rather to maintain its own rules and standards of excellence. Plot and character, scene and tone, diction and syntax and point of view: All of these must be woven into such a seamless whole that the reader attends to the story itself, not to the storyteller. Its governing vision or dominant idea cannot be distilled from the irreducible particulars of the text, as if it were an algebraic equation: Find x. Once the story is turned into a formula centered upon the writer's intentions, it can be tidily packaged and promoted, as with the acolytes, or else scorned and condemned, as with the accusers. Just as divine grace completes and perfects nature, in Aquinas' most famous formula, so does art bring human experience into the order and coherence of the aesthetic form suited to it.

O'Connor understood, almost from the outset, that she had been summoned to this high and difficult vocation. During her first year of study at the University of Iowa Writer's Workshop, twenty-one-year-old Flannery prayed fervently that God would deliver her from mediocrity:

> Help me to get what is more than natural into my work—help me to love & bear with my work on that account. If I have to sweat for it, dear God, let it be as in Your service. I would like to be intelligently holy. . . .
>
> *Maybe I'm mediocre. I'd rather be less. I'd rather be nothing. An imbecile. Yet this is wrong. Mediocrity, if that is my scourge, is something I'll have to submit to.*[7]

O'Connor petitions God for mastery of her craft so that her Christian vision and her literary art might be fused into an irreducible unity. Any division between form and matter produces mediocrity. Their inseparability was made all the more difficult because she sought to write about natural things as they are being made supernatural. The right question, it follows, is whether racism can be found in Flannery O'Connor's fiction, not elsewhere.[8]

7 Flannery O'Connor, *A Prayer Journal*, intro. W. A. Sessions (New York: Farrar, Straus & Giroux, 2013), 18, 27.

8 It is noteworthy that not a single major writer has thus faulted her. In her Massey Lectures at Harvard, for example, Toni Morrison twice praised the excellence of "The Artificial Nigger." She also chided literary critics who "see no connection

Race as a Modern Social Construction

Flannery O'Connor's friend Thomas Gossett was among the first to demonstrate that race is a *modern* social construction. Racial differentiation and discrimination have been endemic to all cultures, but "before the eighteenth century physical differences among peoples were so rarely referred to as a matter of great importance that . . . a case may be made that race consciousness is largely a modern phenomenon."[9] There is neither world enough or time to explain why this should be so. Suffice it to say that it happened in radical repudiation of the ancient Christian witness against racism. St. Paul declares that "God hath made of one blood all nations in the earth to dwell" (Acts 17:26 KJV). St. Augustine is even more forceful:

> But whoever is anywhere born a man, that is, a rational, mortal animal, no matter what unusual appearance he presents in color, movement, sound, nor how peculiar he is in some power, part, or quality of his nature, no Christian can doubt that he springs from that one protoplast. We can distinguish the common human nature from that which is peculiar, and therefore wonderful.[10]

For more than a millennium, there was little if any challenge to monogenesis, the conviction that all human beings spring from a single source, all having been made "in the image and likeness of God." The Catholic Church came close to ending slavery in the thirteenth century. It was then, as Gossett notes, that "we find an indication of how far the Middle Ages were from the idea of race prejudice. In France, Pierre Dubois proposed that more sensible than the Crusades against the Moslem would be intermarriage. Well educated French gentlemen and ladies should marry the Moslem nobility in order to convert them to Christianity and monogamy, and incidentally to pave the way for French domination of the Middle East and Orient" (G, 9).

---

between God's grace and Africanist 'othering' in Flannery O'Connor" (Toni Morrison, *Playing in the Dark: Whiteness and the Literary Imagination* [Cambridge, Mass.: Harvard University Press, 1992], 14, 68).

9 Thomas F. Gossett, *Race: The History of an Idea in America*, new ed. (New York: Oxford University Press, 1997 [1963]), 3. Further references will be paginated within the text as G.

10 *City of God* 4.16.8 (https://www.ccel.org/ccel/schaff/npnf102.iv.XVI.8.html).

Like Gossett, O'Connor marked the seismic Enlightenment shift: "Since the 18th century, the popular spirit of each succeeding age has tended more and more to the view that the ills and mysteries of life will eventually fall before the scientific advances of man" (CW, 815). With this modern victory also came a new confidence in human perfectibility. "It was the hope and belief of the Enlightenment," Gossett writes, "that at birth the mind of a child is a *tabula rasa*, an empty receptacle. Education and environment could make that child into a completely reasonable and intelligent being" (G, 34).[11] Hence O'Connor's complaint that we are now "afflicted with the doctrine of the perfectibility of human nature by its own efforts" (MM, 133).

> The notion of the perfectibility of man came about at the time of the Enlightenment in the 18th century. This is what the South has traditionally opposed. . . . The South . . . still believes that man has fallen and that he is perfectible by God's grace, not by his own unaided efforts. The Liberal approach is that man has never fallen, never incurred guilt, and is ultimately perfectible by his own efforts. Therefore, evil in this light is a problem of better housing, sanitation, health, etc. (HB, 302–3)

This delusion was produced, as we have noticed, by the Enlightenment chimera called "timeless and placeless truth," as if we could view the world *sub specie aeternitatis*—standing above both temporality and spatiality, determining truth apart from convictional communities and narrative traditions. Enlightenment *philosophes* sought to realize the Cartesian dream of becoming masters and possessors of nature. Freed from many of the constraints that once checked and balanced what Augustine called the *libido dominandi*—the desire to exercise domineering power over others—they created categories of control and manipulation. Racial categories were among the most important.

As Gossett observes, secular thinkers began to develop "scientific arguments in favor of the multiple origin of races." Polygenesis replaced monogenesis. Dr. Charles White, an eminent eighteenth-century English physician and surgeon, thus sought to "trace cranial development from

[11] Rayber in *The Violent Bear It Away* and Sheppard in *The Lame Shall Enter First* are imbued with such Enlightenment perfectionism, though they both notably fail to reconstruct the boys whom they seek to reform, Francis Marion Tarwater and Rufus Johnson.

the lower to the higher animals" (G, 47). White's conclusions were typical of his time. Black people, he argued, occupy a station closer to primates than to white people. "In whatever respect the African differs from the European," White wrote, "the particularity brings him nearer to the apes" (R, 49).

In this same century of Enlightenment, Thomas Jefferson declared that "All men are created equal," yet he enslaved more than six hundred blacks during his lifetime, fathering perhaps six children on one of them, Sally Hemings, in an allegedly consensual relation. This is not to make Jefferson the target of easy vilification,[12] but rather to show that Flannery O'Connor was heir not to an ancient but to a thoroughly Enlightenment kind of racism. Hence these questions: Does she embrace this pernicious late-modern racism? Does she treat her black characters as inferior creatures if not semi-primates? Does she deny their innate human dignity and worth? The answer lies in an examination of the characters themselves.

The Racial Manners of O'Connor's Black Characters

I contend that Flannery O'Connor's fiction displays what she called "a single-minded respect for truth" in the manners of her black characters. O'Connor saw the need for racial justice but feared that it was being pushed too hard and too fast, leaving no time for a slowly and mutually developed code of manners whereby blacks and whites might learn to live in amity if not always in charity.

> It requires considerable grace for two races to live together, particularly when the population is divided about fifty-fifty between them and when they have our particular [i.e., violent, even murderous] history. It can't be done without a code of manners based on mutual

[12] "Jefferson wrote that maintaining slavery was like holding 'a wolf by the ear, and we can neither hold him, nor safely let him go.' He thought that his cherished federal union, the world's first democratic experiment, would be destroyed by slavery. To emancipate slaves on American soil, Jefferson thought, would result in a large-scale race war that would be as brutal and deadly as the slave revolt in Haiti in 1791. But he also believed that to keep slaves in bondage, with part of America in favor of abolition and part of America in favor of perpetuating slavery, could only result in a civil war that would destroy the union. Jefferson's latter prediction was correct: in 1861, the contest over slavery sparked a bloody civil war and the creation of two nations—Union and Confederacy—in the place of one" ("Jefferson's Attitudes Toward Slavery," https://www.monticello.org/thomas-jefferson/jefferson-slavery/jefferson-s-attitudes-toward-slavery/).

> charity. . . . When you have a code of manners based on charity, then when the charity fails—as it is going to do constantly—you've got those manners there to preserve each race from small intrusions upon the other. (Quoted in O, 21–22)

It cannot be denied that even the best Southern manners kept blacks in a state of subjection. Among Southerners of moneyed means and political power, regional codes and customs served to fortify white power structures, exacting sure and often severe penalties against blacks who violated them. When Southern social etiquette crossed the lines of race and class, it often worked to preserve a hierarchy of position and privilege: the hegemony of rich over poor, of whites over blacks—even the unworthiest of whites over the worthiest of blacks. The ideal of *noblesse oblige* called for the privileged ones at the top to treat the hapless ones at the bottom with both courtesy and charity. Yet there could be no fundamental breach of the system itself.

The "Signifying" Manners of Southern Blacks

Because they were enslaved for centuries, Southern blacks created their own elaborate and subtle system of manners, a way of holding their alleged superiors at a critical distance, subtly but surely with irony. It is called "signifying"—i.e., offering seeming deference to whites while in fact making raucous ridicule of them. One of the most telling examples of such black ironizing occurs in "Revelation." There the self-congratulating Ruby Turpin[13] meets her awful comeuppance when a Wellesley sophisticate named Mary Grace slugs her in the eye with a huge social-science textbook, flings her to the floor, grabs her by the throat, then whispers into her ear, "Go back to hell where you came from, you old warthog!" (CW, 646). Mrs. Turpin is outraged, of course, that such a thing could happen to such an upright woman, much less that her Lord would allow it.

Mary Grace's epithet rankles. Unable to confess it to anyone else, Ruby seeks sympathy from a group of black women farmhands. When she tells them what happened, they affect the utmost sympathy, when of course

[13] Mrs. Turpin drifts off to sleep at night by counting her blessings, naming them one by one, imagining the kind of person she might have been if she were not her own splendid self. Chief among these divinely bestowed gifts would have been Jesus' decision not to make her a trashy white woman. Ruby is confident, instead, that he "would have made her a neat clean respectable Negro woman, herself but black" (CW, 636).

they are making merciless mockery of her. The result is one of the funniest scenes in all of O'Connor's work:

> "Hi come she do that"? the old woman asked. "What ail her?"
>
> "She sho shouldn't said nothin ugly to you. . . . You so sweet. You the sweetest lady I know."
>
> "She pretty too," the one with the hat on said.
>
> "And stout," the other one said. "I never knowed no sweeter white lady."
>
> "That's the truth befo' Jesus," the old woman said. "Amen! You des as sweet and pretty as you can be." . . .
>
> "Where she at?" the youngest woman cried in a piercing voice [referring to Mrs. Turpin's accuser].
>
> "Lemme see her. I'll kill her!"
>
> "I'll killer with you!" the other one cried.
>
> "She b'long in the sylum," the old woman said emphatically. "You the sweetest white lady I know."
>
> "She pretty too," the other two said. "Stout as she can be and sweet. Jesus satisfied with her!"
>
> "Deed he is," the old woman declared. (CW, 650)

Ruby Turpin knows, of course, that these alleged compliments are sugary insults. She knows also that "stout" does not mean strong and muscular but plump bordering on obese. That these women could have identified sweeter *black* ladies must have been especially galling. Mrs. Turpin "knew just exactly how much Negro flattery was worth and it added to her rage." "Idiots! [she] growled to herself. You could never say anything intelligent to a nigger. You could talk at them but not with them" (CW, 650). It never occurs to Ruby Turpin that she can have no common life with her black workers since she never bothers even to learn their names—only to identify them as old, young, hatted, and so forth. Anonymous though they remain, they have mocked her racial pretense to scorn.

Randall and Morgan as Clever Mockers of Asbury Fox in "The Enduring Chill"

Such wickedly double-edged humor is also rampant in "The Enduring Chill." It concerns the return of Asbury Fox from New York City to his rural Georgia home in order to gather material for a play he is writing about "the Negro." Nowhere is his mother's alleged racism made more evident, according to Asbury, than in her refusal to allow Randall and

Morgan, the black farm hands, to drink the abundant milk. Fox seeks to celebrate a secular sacrament with these supposedly submissive blacks by imbibing freely from this nutritious font.[14] "It [would be] one of those moments of communion when the difference between black and white is absorbed into nothing" (CW, 558). These uncultured black men know, as the sophisticate Asbury does not, that to drink unpasteurized milk is to court undulant fever, a serious lifelong though not fatal disease. And so they let him drink his fill of the potentially noxious liquid, all the while making fun of Fox's moral pretense, having no doubt heard that "to spare the rod is to spoil the child."[15]

> "Howcome you let him drink all that milk every day?" [Morgan asks]
> "What he do is him," Randall said. "What I do is me."
> "Howcome he talks so ugly about his ma?" [Morgan again asks]
> "She ain't whup him enough when he was little," Randall said. (CW, 560)

Randall and Morgan get a last chance to prod the wan and sickly Asbury with the needle-prick of their "signifying." Thinking himself to be mortally ill, he asks that they be brought to his bedside for a final farewell.

> The two of them came in grinning and shuffled to the side of the bed. They stood there, Randall in front and Morgan behind. "You sho do look well," Randall said. "You looks very well."
> "You looks well," the other one said. "Yessuh, you looks fine."
> "I ain't ever seen you looking so well before," Randall said. . . .
> "Yessuh," Randall said, "I speck you ain't even sick." . . .
> "I'm about to die," Asbury said irritably.
> "You looks fine," Randall said.
> "You be up and around in a few days," Morgan predicted. . . .
> "I speck you might have a little cold," Randall said after a time.
> "I takes a little sugar and turpentine when I has a cold," Morgan said. . . .
> "We be going," Randall said. "You sho do look well."
> "You sho does," Morgan said. (CW, 569–70)

14 Like Ruby Turpin, Asbury Fox cannot distinguish one from the other, even addressing Morgan as "boy," a slur-word perhaps worse even than the n-word.

15 It is not an actual biblical injunction but an adaptation of Prov 13:24 (KJV): "He that spareth his rod hateth his son: but he that loveth him chasteneth him betimes."

Julian's Kind Mother Versus Her Mean Counterpart

A far more controversial example of Flannery O'Connor's depiction of racial conflict occurs in "Everything That Rises Must Converge." Julian the protagonist is a white liberal who turns a rightful demand for racial justice into a wrongful demand for moral congratulation. To demonstrate his own liberation, he deliberately occupies a bus bench next to a black man who instantly penetrates his pretense. Seeing that Julian seeks to use him for the practice of his own moral hygiene, he immediately moves to another seat.[16] Julian is so obsessed with casting out the racist motes in his mother's eye that he remains blind to the log-sized presumption and ingratitude that blinker his own vision. Julian can "love" the anonymous black person whom he does not know, but not the mother whom he does know and who also knows him (cf. 1 John 4:20).

As often happens in O'Connor's stories, liberated offspring prove to be more egregious sinners than unprogressive parents. Having come down in the world economically, and thus forced to live in scrimping sacrifice of her own needs to meet Julian's, his mother continues to support her ne'er-do-well live-at-home son. Though conventionally prejudiced about blacks, she is capable of the love that matters most: She cares deeply about her uncaring son. Despite her verbal scorn for blacks, she is not a mean-minded racist. For while she can disparage blacks in general, she never mistreats anyone in particular.[17]

[16] Sarah Gordon has shown that this story derives directly from O'Connor's correspondence with Maryat Lee concerning a bus ride that Lee made from Milledgeville back to New York. In an attempted gesture of human solidarity with a victim of racial injustice, Lee had sat beside a black woman who was wearing a purple hat and who was burdened with a fussy child. Perhaps sensing what was self-seeking in such white "charity," the black woman removed herself to a distant seat as soon as she could, Lee reported. Gordon notes that the limits of Lee's own liberalism became evident when, exasperated by the black woman's refusal to honor her act of good will, Lee called her a "bitch" (Sarah Gordon, "Maryat and Julian and the 'Not So Bloodless Revolution,'" *Flannery O'Connor Bulletin* 21 [1992]: 32).

[17] In this regard, she is not unlike Regina Cline O'Connor. Flannery would warn guests not to bring up the race question in the presence of her mother, lest it propel her racial locomotive onto a track that had no stopping places. At the same time, Mrs. O'Connor's regard for individual blacks was remarkable. When one of the black farm workers suffered a back injury, Mrs. O'Connor not only visited the nearby house where he lived but also gave him a liniment rubdown in an unthinkable act of cross-racial intimacy.

A sales clerk had sold Julian's mother a hat in the assurance that it would set her apart from everyone else. Yet soon after purchasing it, she encounters a black woman wearing an identical hat. Far from being angered or even embarrassed, Julian's mother quietly accepts what Julian hoped would be her humiliation. Near the story's end, she again confronts this black woman together with her young son Carver. In complete innocence, the kind white lady plays peek-a-boo with Carver. The child reciprocates such jovial affection by sitting next to her rather than his own mother. In a further gesture of glad-heartedness, Julian's mother gives the boy a shiny copper as she leaves the bus. The child's mother is infuriated. Blinded by a rage that is unable to distinguish a kind from a condescending gesture, the black woman strikes Julian's mother to the ground, giving her a fatal stroke.

Some readers have seen the penny-giving gesture as a quintessential racist act. Thus have they justified the black woman's violent response. Wanting their ethical categories to remain pristine, these interpreters cannot countenance the moral complexity that O'Connor knew to be the stuff of life and thus of fiction. To view the gift of the shiny copper as anything other than an innocent gesture is to indulge in the same virtue-signaling moralism that Julian pours on his mother as she lies fatally stricken by the black *furiosa*: "'Don't think that was just an uppity Negro woman,' [Julian] said. 'That was the whole colored race which will no longer take your condescending pennies. . . . What all this means,' he said, 'is that the old world is gone. The old manners are obsolete and your graciousness is not worth a damn. . . . You needn't act as if the world has come to an end,' he said, 'because it hasn't. From now on you've got to live in a new world and face a few realities for a change. Buck up,' he said, 'it won't kill you'" (CW, 499–500).

Julian's mother does in fact die, but her death is not due to an unrepentant racism, nor is it due entirely to the blow struck by the violent black woman. She dies, instead, from the self-righteousness of her own son. For the sake of an abstract sense of justice, he has denied the most fundamental of all loves: the filial love for the mother who has not only birthed him but also nourished his feckless youth.

O'Connor ends the story with a searing scene. It is imbued not only with Julian's regret but with a glimmer of hope for him:

> He turned her over. Her face was fiercely distorted. One eye, large and staring, moved slightly to the left as if it had become unmoored.

> The other remained fixed on him, raked his face again, found nothing and closed.
>
> "Wait here, wait here!" he cried and jumped up and began to run for help toward a cluster of lights he saw in the distance ahead of him. "Help, help!" he shouted, but his voice was thin, scarcely a thread of sound. The lights drifted farther away the faster he ran and his feet moved numbly as if they carried him nowhere. The tide of darkness seemed to sweep him back to her, postponing from moment to moment his entry into the world of guilt and sorrow. (CW, 500)[18]

Even as she dies, Julian's addled mother remains gracious rather than resentful. Hallucinating, she calls out for Caroline, the black nurse from her childhood, perhaps remembering that she provided the unqualified love that her own son had refused to grant.

Three Signal Moments in "The Artificial Nigger"[19]

Flannery O'Connor repeatedly singled out "The Artificial Nigger" as her favorite story. The title itself has led to its banning from most secondary and collegiate classrooms. John Crowe Ransom, the distinguished literary critic and editor of the *Kenyon Review*, urged O'Connor to change the title before it appeared in a 1955 issue, knowing well that would give offense. She refused: "I stood up for my title." For her to have sanitized it would have robbed the story of its enormous power, the power to transform a racist slur into an anti-racist redemption. It occurs in the lives of a grandfather named Mr. Head and his grandson Nelson. They dwell alone in the

18 O'Connor does not romanticize underprivileged blacks. In "The Displaced Person," Astor and Sulk are no-count farmhands who repeatedly reinforce the whining complacency of Mrs. MacIntyre, the story's protagonist. She owns the dairy farm that is now managed by Mr. Guizac, a Polish refugee who has made it flourish. She determines, utterly without cause, to get rid of him. Why? Not, as it might seem, because Mrs. McIntyre is outraged upon hearing of his plan to rescue a niece from Polish oppression in the only legal way possible—by bringing her as a bride to marry a black youth who works on the farm. The subtle truth is that Mrs. McIntyre is scandalized by Guizac's excellence and efficiency. He robs her of her moaning self-pity, and so he must be done away with. In the only O'Connor scene akin to a crucifixion, pure-souled Guizac is crushed and killed by a runaway tractor. Everyone sees what's happening, but they all fail to scream in horror. "She had felt her eyes and Mr. Shortley's eyes and the Negro's eyes come together in one look that froze them in collusion forever" (CW, 325–26).

19 The following paragraphs are a précis of my full treatment of the story in *Flannery O'Connor and the Christ-Haunted South*, 143–53.

remote reaches of northern Georgia. In their lonely isolation, they should have been bound by the blessed ties of familial mutuality. Instead, they are infected with the aboriginal Adamic evil that we have heard St. Augustine name as the *libido dominandi*, the desire to dominate. Yet at three crucial turning points in the story, they are proffered potential moments for healing their lust for power over each other—all three coming from black characters.

A Black Man Who Exemplifies Regal Dignity

The first occasion occurs on a train ride to Atlanta. Mr. Head wants to show Nelson that the impersonal city is an alien place, not least of all because it is full of "niggers." Once ten-year-old Nelson learns to loathe Georgia's capital, he will want to remain on their rural farm, the better to care for his sixty-year-old grandfather when he becomes old and needy. Soon after they have boarded the train bound for the city, a light-complexioned black man strides majestically past them in a steady gait. He is followed by two young women of similar hue, perhaps his granddaughters, as if they were slowly walking in a royal procession. He has a small white mustache and crinkly white hair. With one hand resting on his ample paunch, the "coffee-colored" man uses his other hand to pick up and set down his cane. This "tremendous Negro," as the narrator calls him, is clearly prosperous. He wears a buttoned suit complemented by a satin tie as well as a ruby stick-pin and sapphire ring. He also has "a heavy sad face and his neck [bulges] over his white collar on either side." (CW, 217). Yet he is not enraged at having to walk the length of the train from the black carriage at the back to the segregated dining car at the front. Rather than chafing at his unjust fate, he maintains a quiet but proud dignity.

No sooner has the entourage passed by them than Mr. Head decides to entrap Nelson in his ignorance of blacks. He thus asks the youth what he has seen. "A man," Nelson replies. Oblivious to racial distinctions, the boy instinctively discerns what he cannot articulate: a race-transcending instance of our common humanity. Mr. Head will not abide such truth. He pounces—humiliating Nelson for failing to detect "his first nigger." Far from being paragon of youthful innocence, Nelson is furious at his grandfather for allegedly tricking him: "You said they were black. . . . You never said they were tan." Yet the boy aims his fury not at his grandfather, but at the chocolate-colored figure for failing to be obviously black: "He felt that the Negro had deliberately walked down the aisle in order to make a fool of him and he hated him with a fierce raw fresh hate" (CW, 216). Yet O'Connor is offering no lesson in Civics 101: "Rather than being instinctive, racial contempt must be taught." Of such obvious sociological truth, subtle art is never made.

A Black Woman Who Inspires Marian Longings

This second episode occurs when Nelson becomes separated from his uncle and thus lost in one of Atlanta's ghettos. The boy wants to cry out for help in getting back into the train station in the center of the city, but no one is present to hear him except a large black woman leaning in her doorway. It matters not to Nelson that she insults him, telling him "You in town now" and calling him Sugarpie. He feels "as if a cool spray had been turned on him."

> He stood drinking in every detail of her. His eyes traveled up from her great knees to her forehead and then made a triangular path from the glistening sweat on her neck down and across her tremendous bosom and over her bare arm back to where her fingers lay hidden in her hair. He suddenly wanted her to reach down and pick him up and draw him against her and then he wanted to feel her breath on his face. He wanted to look down and down into her eyes while she held him tighter and tighter. He had never had such a feeling before. He felt as if he were reeling down through a pitchblack tunnel. . . . Nelson would have collapsed at her feet if Mr. Head had not pulled him roughly away. "You act like you don't have any sense!" the old man growled. (CW, 223)

Though only ten, Nelson is not immune to sexual stirrings. Yet O'Connor is no unconfessed Freudian. This motherless child longs not only for an earthly mother's sweet caress but also for the gracious embrace of a black Madonna, which she surely is.

A Black Sambo Who Becomes a Crucifix

The third and far most important moment of redemption provided by a black figure occurs near the end of the story. Nelson and Mr. Head have become hopelessly alienated in terrible violations of each other. They seem set to dwell forever in the hell of mutual recrimination. Lost both morally and spatially, they happen upon a black lawn jockey in front of a Southern mansion. This plaster travesty is a Sambo-figure holding a slice of watermelon, as if blacks were capable of little else than cheap gratification of their appetites. He is supposed to be a smiling and carefree "darky," but he has a chipped eye, he lurches forward at an awkward angle, and the watermelon has turned brown. This "Negro jocko" is a gross annunciation that black lives do not matter. "It was not possible," declares O'Connor's narrator, "to tell if the artificial Negro were meant to be young or old; he looked too miserable to be either" (CW, 229).

As backwater creatures dwelling virtually unto themselves, Nelson and Mr. Head perhaps have never entered a Church, and certainly they have never encountered a crucifix. Even so, they instinctively recognize its black equivalent. They are riveted by this emblem of suffering and shame, as it becomes the instrument of their unexpected and undeserved reconciliation.

> The two of them stood there with their necks forward almost at the same angle and their shoulders curved in almost exactly the same way and their hands trembling identically in their pockets. Mr. Head looked like an ancient child and Nelson like a miniature old man. They stood gazing at the artificial Negro as if they were faced with some great mystery, some monument to another's victory that brought them together in common defeat. They could both feel it dissolving their differences like an action of mercy. Mr. Head had never known before what mercy felt like because he had been too good to deserve any, but he felt he knew now. (CW, 230)

Though it will take months, even years, to work out their salvation in fear and trembling, they have at least embarked on the right road—as, yet again, a black figure has been made central to Flannery O'Connor's fiction. This time he is not a mocker of white pretense but a mediator of divine mercy.

Buford Munson: A Brown Man Who Saves a White Boy

Buford Munson appears in the opening sentence of *The Violent Bear It Away*, and he is present again in the novel's penultimate paragraph.[20] He

[20] To her credit, Angela O'Donnell treats this scene with both care and insight, noting that "Buford possesses power, authenticity, and authority—all of which [young] Tarwater lacks. He schools the boy in the ways of being human and holy, speaking to him without fear and without guile. This is no pantomime. In fact, if anyone is lesser in human terms, it is the white man" (O, 138).

is clearly a figure of signal importance. We first meet him when he and his wife[21] approach Powderhead in order to buy jugs of old Mason's illicit whiskey. Munson had actually come there earlier, laboring from noon until sundown to provide the reverent burial that the old prophet had demanded—"in a decent and Christian way, with the sign of [the] Saviour at the head of the grave and enough dirt on top to keep the dogs from digging it up" (CW, 331). Munson's wife is genuinely grieved at the old prophet's passing. She "lifted her head and let out a low sustained wail, piercing and formal." On the previous two nights, she had a dream-vision of Mason's dead body, though his spirit remained restless because his corpse had not been properly buried. Buford interprets his wife's dream as being prompted by their intimate knowledge of the ancient seer; he was not a stranger to them but an honored neighbor. It is noteworthy that Munson speaks not in degrading black dialect but in standard if countrified English: "'He been predicting his passing for many years,' Buford said. . . . 'I known him well. I known him very well indeed.'" Precisely because he has not "known" the elder Tarwater well enough to discern his knotty integrity, young Tarwater responds to Mrs. Munson's grief with racist contempt: "'Tell her to shut up that. . . . I'm in charge here now and don't want no nigger-mourning'" (CW, 357).

When the rebel youth returns to Powderhead at the end, Munson does not greet him as the prodigal who has penitently returned home. Instead, he rends Tarwater with merciless judgment, "with a scorn that could penetrate any surface." Nor is Munson self-effacing about his own faithfulness over against the boy's apostasy: "It's owing to me he's resting there. I buried him while you were laid out drunk. It's owing to me his corn has been plowed. It's owing to me the sign of his Saviour is over his head" (CW, 477). Without Munson's reverent act, Francis Marion Tarwater would have been consumed with unpardonable guilt for incinerating his elderly uncle in a fiery refusal of the old prophet's commission to serve as his successor. Thus is Munson the material means of the youth's spiritual salvation.

Yet he is much more, as becomes evident in the novel's final scenes, which are imbued with a numinous mystery rarely if ever surpassed in O'Connor's fiction. When Tarwater first sees Munson back at Powderhead,

[21] They are never identified as such, though their marital relation is clearly implied. As the Munsons make their path to what had been old Mason's home, he lets her lead, gently touching her elbow rather than harshly insisting that she trail behind him.

he is astride a mule in majestic statuary stillness: "the two might have been made out of rock" (CW, 476). Initially, the white boy greets the brown man with a clenched fist of threat, but when he sees the rugged cross that Munson had planted in the raw ground, "the boy's hands opened stiffly as if he were dropping something he had been clutching all his life" (CW, 477). At last he is loosening his grip on his self-damning pride. And in a final act of mutuality, Munson even partially enters young Tarwater's ultimate moment of grace, in a fine understated description:

> The Negro sat watching [the boy's] strange spent face and grew uneasy. The skin across it tightened as he watched and the eyes, lifting beyond the grave, appeared to see something coming in the distance. Buford turned his head. The darkening field behind him stretched downward toward the woods. When he looked back again, the boy's vision seemed to pierce the very air. The Negro trembled and felt suddenly a pressure on him too great to bear. He sensed it as a burning in the atmosphere. His nostrils twitched. He muttered something and turned the mule around and moved off, across the back field and down to the woods. (CW, 477)

Munson is so spiritually keen that he can sense, with appropriate agony, the holy gravity descending on young Tarwater as he mystically envisions the old prophet feasting at the heavenly Banquet.

Coleman Parrum as a Black Man of Transcendent Self-Restraint

Nearing the end of her brief life, Flannery O'Connor broke fresh ground even as she was dying. She had dealt with race relations throughout her fiction, always seeking to avoid the easy binaries that damned white victimizers and pitied black victims. Thus had she satirized archly righteous race-reformers, especially Julian in "Everything That Rises Must Converge" and Sheppard in "The Lame Shall Enter First."[22] Yet critique alone would not finally suffice. Something positive and revolutionary was required.[23] In her posthumously published final story—the unpolished typescript was found on her desk—she took a remarkable turn indeed:

[22] I have sought to show why O'Connor was finally dissatisfied with her attack on Sheppard. See "Why Flannery O'Connor Had Doubts About 'The Lame Shall Enter First,'" *Mississippi Quarterly* 17, no. 1 (Autumn 2024).

[23] In *Why Do the Heathen Rage?* she had sought but eventually abandoned what was virtually impossible, at least in O'Connor's world—to have a white man marry a black woman. Jessica Hooten Wilson attempts to give narrative order to

She set a black man and a white man in an intimate cross-racial friendship, having them live together for thirty years in amity if not equity. As if in repentance for the shallow artistry and naïve moralism of "The Geranium," her first published story, she used her flagging energies to radically recast it in "Judgment Day."[24]

The two central scenes involve Coleman Parrum and T. C. Tanner. As the sickly white master of a remote Georgia logging operation, Tanner has established emblematic authority over his black workers by carving figurines that become virtual fetishes to them, even as his knife serves also to warn that he could bury its blade in their gut if he catches them slacking. A drunken black man named Coleman Parrum wanders into this conventional Southern scene wherein white privilege and power serve to dominate poor and submissive blacks. Yet even in his sorry inebriated state, Coleman seems to pose a threat to the labors of his black brothers. Hence Tanner's determination to be rid of Coleman by the usual threat of white violence: "Nigger, this knife is in my hand now, but if you ain't out of my sight . . ." (CW, 682). Parrum surely knows that this weak white man is no match for him, and that he could easily kill Tanner, even though he would surely be caught and prosecuted, perhaps even lynched.

The story's crucial turn occurs when Tanner fashions a pair of lensless spectacles by attaching bits of wire to a piece of pine bark carved with two openings. He then commands Coleman to wear them—as if to confirm that he is yet another stupid and submissive "nigger." Coleman dutifully complies, peering back at Tanner through these glasses that have no glass. Yet far from being an act of supine submission, it is one of the most stunning moments in all of O'Connor's fiction. For Coleman chooses not to slay but to enter into a surprising communion with his sneering white master. Thirty years after the fact, Tanner can still recall "the exact instant in the muddy liquor-swollen eyes when the pleasure of having a knife in this white man's gut was balanced against something else, he could not tell what" (CW, 683).

What was it? O'Connor's narrator answers with clarity and depth: Coleman had discerned their common humanity. He "had an instant's sensation of seeing before him a negative image of himself, as if clownishness and captivity had been their common lot" (CW, 683). Thus is Coleman

---

the manifold drafts of this bootless enterprise in *Flannery O'Connor's* Why Do the Heathen Rage? (Grand Rapids: Brazos, 2024).

[24] I offer a full treatment of the two stories in *Flannery O'Connor and the Christ-Haunted South*, 134–42.

transcendently restrained, even in his alcohol-addled state, by a suprahuman revelation. He sees that he and his white "master" are trapped in a ridiculous alienation. Only if they can break free from such bondage can they find true friendship. Though it is not fully realized for thirty years, O'Connor artistically prepares for it by having Tanner ponder his burial in the opening scene. As with so many of her other stories, this one will end in death.

Too proud to remain with Tanner on property newly purchased by a prosperous black man—his friendship with Coleman not giving him an equally high regard for others of his race—he has fled to New York City to live with his daughter. There his health continues to deteriorate as he soon suffers a stroke. Bereft of companionship with Coleman, he seeks to befriend the black actor who lives next door. He affectionately addresses him as "Preacher," assuming him to be a fellow believer exiled from the neighborly South to the alien North. The anti-Christian actor is outraged—"I'm not a preacher! I don't believe that crap. There ain't no Jesus and there ain't no God." Undaunted by such rank apostasy, Tanner makes his stern Christian counter-witness: "And you ain't black and I ain't white" (CW, 690). The actor responds by slamming the dying old man against a wall, pulling his hat over his face, then thrusting his head and arms between the spokes of the banister. He looks almost like a Rouault crucifixion. Yet this is no pity-prompting scene, since Tanner has faithfully prepared for his death and deliverance: "The Lord is my shepherd," he muttered, "I shall not want" (CW, 693).

In a quasi-mystical dream vision, Tanner imagines his body being taken back to Georgia—back *home* in both the proximate and ultimate sense. Still clownish but no longer captive, he will leap from his rickety casket, shouting proudly to Coleman and his friend Hooten, "Judgment Day! Judgment Day! You idiots didn't know it was Judgment Day, did you?" (CW, 694). For Flannery O'Connor, God's judgment is surely Yes rather than No to T. C. Tanner, a man who was set on the road to his redemption by the transcendent self-restraint of Coleman Parrum. Such black characters are the true measure of Flannery O'Connor's splendid literary contribution to the vexed question of race in America.

Conclusion

When in 1971 I finished graduate school at the University of Chicago and took my first teaching post at Wake Forest University in North Carolina, I was all set to come home to my native South and to begin wiping the grins off fundamentalist faces. I was prepared to rub pious Baptist noses in the cold snows of modern secularity, so that my students would become church-transcending sophisticates like me. I had learned from Paul Tillich that modern secular culture poses questions to which theology provides answers. Tillich called it the "method of correlation." It is far from a negligible enterprise. Yet it is difficult to stake one's existence on the proposition that "culture is the form of religion and religion is the substance of culture."

Even so, I remained a slow starter. During my very first semester, I taught several literary "masters of suspicion," as Paul Ricoeur named such writers—Hemingway and Faulkner, Kafka and Lawrence and Camus. I faced, however, a serious problem. There was not, alas, a single fundamentalist to be found! My classrooms were filled, instead, with bright young products of the secularizing Sixties, many of them having protested the Vietnam War and experimented with drugs. They were often poorly catechized Catholics coming down from the North, or else regional Protestants knowing little about their own Christian tradition.

I was at wit's end. I had been educated for a job that I was grossly unprepared to perform. How could I deepen and revitalize the faith—not only of my students, but chiefly of myself? Yet I was still under the illusion that the great monuments of Western art and culture were sufficient to sustain Christian culture even as the churches lost their influence. An academic year spent in Italy, 1976–1977, cured me of this notion. The majestic European cathedrals were on their way to becoming museums, even as their civil impact was also dwindling. And so I plunged into the work of Søren Kierkegaard, seeking to find a radical alternative to the collapse of Christendom that he had so acutely diagnosed in the nineteenth century. Eventually I discovered what Kierkegaard himself confessed—that he was a corrective rather than a cure, a waystation and not a terminus.

At first, I resisted the curative called Karl Barth. I quailed at the prospect of tackling even a small portion of the massive thirteen volumes and 9,257 pages of Barth's masterwork with its forbidding title: *Church Dogmatics*. Yet after an arduous self-tutelage in Barth, I began setting his theology in relation to a clutch of writers who helped re-baptize my own imagination as well to reinvigorate the dormant Christianity of my students: Augustine and Dante, Luther and Calvin, Herbert and Donne, Bunyan and the Wesleys, Dickinson and Hopkins, Dostoevsky and Solzhenitsyn, Eliot and Auden, Tolkien and Lewis, Graham Greene and Walker Percy, Charles Williams and Dorothy L. Sayers—while also discovering the Icon tradition of Eastern Christianity during my final years. Best of all, I returned to Flannery O'Connor. She arrested the attention of my students like no one else. For all fifty years in the collegiate classroom, therefore, I devoted myself to teaching these radically Christian authors to my remarkably receptive students.

Even my friendly critics sometimes complain that, as an unordained Baptist who has not found anyone willing to lay hands on him, I am not the interpreter so much as the preacher of Flannery O'Connor. To which I reply: "Guilty as charged. Now show me a better text." This is more than a snarky dismissal. I have dedicated this book to her memory because I cannot fathom what my life would have become without first encountering her work when I was a senior at East Texas State. Paul Barrus, my excellent English professor and director of my 1965 master's thesis on O'Connor, was the only Roman Catholic on the faculty at our small college located in the Blackland prairie town of Commerce. He sponsored O'Connor's visit to our campus in November 1962. This event became a moment of no return, an irreversible rounding of a corner. I can bring no greater tribute to Flannery O'Connor, therefore, than to confess that she has restored my life in the visible Church.

ACKNOWLEDGMENTS

The genesis of this book is rooted in my boyhood. I was raised during the 1950s in the First Baptist Church of Linden, Texas, a county-seat town (pop. 1744) located among rolling hills, piney woods, and small streams. My pastor was Joe Gilmore—not Joseph, but just plain Joe. He was the only Baylor graduate ever to serve as our preacher. Among the other fine folks who shaped me, Gilmore stood apart. His library was well stocked, and he preached thoughtful sermons. Above all else, he wrestled with a book that was no antique tribal anthology, no literary masterpiece penned by consummate artists, not one book among other books, but the rough-hewn and scandalous Book called the Bible. I wanted to be like him.

Because of Gilmore's preaching and ministry, this Baptist church became my Magnetic North. This was not altogether unusual. *Not* to have been shaped by Baptist life amid the Bible Belt would have been the real anomaly. My little community numbered four or five Baptist churches. Yet there were no Presbyterians, Episcopalians, or Lutherans—and not a single Roman Catholic parish in the entire county. As we say in eastern Texas, there are more Baptists than people. Like cats, we multiply by fighting. One Baptist, a believer; two Baptists, a church; three Baptists, a church split.

To describe my Baptist formation as fundamentalist would be ludicrous. We never spoke of the Bible as inerrant in its science and history, or as infallible in its verbal inspiration. These strange terms were unknown to us. They were Yankee and urban delusions. We believed the Bible because it was true, because its narrative was shaping us into the people we were meant—though we often failed miserably—to be. We read it and heard it preached as the world's true Story: from the original and continuing Creation of the cosmos, through the aboriginal Calamity that brought sin and death into the world, further still to the cruciform Corrective that recreates the world in Israel and Christ and the Church, until the final Consummation in the life to come, where we shall meet God face to face. Baptists like alliteration.

This overarching Christian narrative, with its calamitous stories and drastic doctrines, shaped me perhaps more powerfully in its music than its biblical texts. I still find myself singing its hymns in times of great distress and even greater joyfulness. These are some of the blood-soaked, atonement-driven, heaven-aimed gospel songs that shaped me: "We're Marching to Zion" ("beautiful, beautiful Zion"); "Bringing in the Sheaves" ("we shall come rejoicing, bringing in the sheaves"); "When We All Get to Heaven" ("what rejoicing there will be"); "Are You Washed in the Blood of the Lamb" ("the precious blood of the lamb"); "There Is a Fountain Filled with Blood" ("drawn from Immanuel's veins"); "Blessed Assurance" ("Jesus is mine; Oh, what a foretaste of glory divine"); "I Will Arise and Go to Jesus" ("He will embrace me in his arms"); "Just a Closer Walk with Thee" ("Grant it, Jesus, is my plea. Daily walking close to Thee. Let it be, dear Lord, let it be"); "I Am a Poor Wayfaring Stranger" ("just passing through this world below"); "What Can Wash Away My Sins" ("nothing but the blood of Jesus"); "Have Thine Own Way, Lord" ("Thou art the potter, I am the clay"); and, above all others, "Just as I Am" ("without one plea, but that thy blood was shed for me, and that thou bidst me come to thee, O Lamb of God, I come, I come"). These Gospel songs, this reading and preaching of Bible, permanently marked me. They gave me the most important thing in the world: the Gospel of Jesus Christ, his Church, and his Kingdom.

Fast forward to 1977, a quarter century later. I was on a research leave from Wake Forest to study in Florence, hoping to improve my chicken-fried Italian so I could read Dante in his own tongue. I met weekly with a tutor to explicate a few cantos of the *Divine Comedy*. My teacher was a polyglot linguist who, at age twenty-four, had earned a doctorate in Romance Languages at Johns Hopkins. I held her in justified awe. Yet at the end of one particular session, she paused to ask a question: "I know that you and Larry Cunningham [the Notre Dame friend who had recommended her] are great admirers of Flannery O'Connor, but I can't make heads or tails of her." I was struck with a lightning-bolt revelation. I suddenly discerned that, whereas my Florentine teacher knew perhaps four or five other languages than her own, I had received a different gift altogether: My Baptist youth had given me the scandal of the Gospel and thus opened my eyes to the scandalous witness of Flannery O'Connor.

My fellow travelers along the O'Connor Road have been too numerous to acknowledge adequately. At Baylor, my main O'Connor companions have included Barry Harvey, Richard Russell, David Lyle Jeffrey, and Fr. Timothy Vaverek, as well as graduate assistants Jonathan Speegle and Rachel Toombs. John Sykes and Jim McCoy were my first O'Connor-inspired students at Wake Forest in the mid-1970s. John Hayes and Pete Candler followed a decade later. Flannery's friends Tom and Louise Gossett were my academic colleagues in Winston-Salem. Pat Johansson and I team-taught a course on O'Connor and Percy at Wake Forest. Hank Edmondson and I joined the late Bill Sessions as unindicted co-conspirators at several O'Connor conferences. Vigen Guroian provided a fine Eastern Orthodox perspective on O'Connor's work. Jordan Rowan Fannin, Daniel Train, Jessica Hooten Wilson, and Rachel Toombs all wrote strong doctoral dissertations on O'Connor under my direction.

I have greatly benefited from the work of such fellow O'Connor specialists as Frederick Asals, Ben Alexander, Jill Baumgaertner, Jean Cash, Robert Donahoo, John Desmond, Bruce Gentry, Sarah Gordon, Christina Bieber Lake, Rosemary Magee, Angela Alaimo O'Donnell, Farrell O'Gorman, Jonathan Rogers, Henry Russell, and Susan Srigley. Tom Haddox from the University of Tennessee has been my main conversation partner during my Knoxville years. Louise Florencourt, Flannery O'Connor's first cousin, welcomed me on my several visits to Milledgeville and Andalusia, the O'Connor farm. Her sister Frances Florencourt has been indispensable as well. It was an honor also to know Sally Fitzgerald, O'Connor's close friend and authoritative editor of the *Collected Works* in the Library of America series. I have learned much from the scores of students who have taken my O'Connor-laden courses at Wake Forest and Baylor as well as Providence College. I am also indebted to participants in my two summer seminars on O'Connor at Regent College in Vancouver, especially to Megan Ramsey, who first pointed out that Flannery O'Connor's self-portrait is modeled on the sixth-century icon of Christ Pantocrator from the Mt. Sinai monastery. Jenny Hunt has generously served as my long-suffering production manager at the Baylor University Press, performing many acts of supererogation—i.e., righteous deeds above those necessary for her own salvation—in my behalf.

I can never be sufficiently grateful to Ed Wilson, the Wake Forest provost who hired me in 1971 and who strongly supported me during my twenty-six years there. Rowan Williams, the former Archbishop of Canterbury, has also affirmed my work on Flannery O'Connor over the years. In *Grace and Necessity*, he taught me that the loving God at work in her fiction fills her characters with passions and longings that are almost too cruelly painful to bear. To do anything less would make him less than the God of Jesus Christ and his visible Church.

Among my many other unpayable debts, by far the greatest is owed to Warren Carr, pastor of the Wake Forest Baptist Church during my formative years on the faculty, 1971–1985. Carr was at once smarter, wiser, and funnier than most of the professors. He was also the most courageous. Because of his preaching on race, his church in Durham had been desecrated and a Molotov cocktail had been thrown onto the roof of the parsonage, though it failed to explode. Undeterred, Carr unflinchingly insisted that, while black Christians were not the social and cultural equals of his white members, they were their brothers and sisters in Christ. Yet he never turned his churches into clubs of the racially righteous. He refused to instrumentalize the Gospel for the sake of any allegedly greater good, proclaiming instead that Jesus transforms and redeems the best moral causes as well as the worst moral evils. He was unabashedly committed to Christ and his visible Church. There alone, he preached, can we be reconciled to each other because God has reconciled himself to us. I cannot fathom what my life would be without his witness.

Permissions

An earlier version of "How the Church Became Invisible: A Christian Reading of American Literary Tradition" (cowritten with Stanley Hauerwas) was published in *Invisible Conversations: Religion in the Literature of America*, ed. Roger Lundin (Waco, Tex.: Baylor University Press, 2009), 159–86, 210–16.

A different version of "Flannery O'Connor's Self-Portrait in the Light of Christ Pantocrator" appeared in *Touchstone: A Journal of Mere Christianity* 36, no. 5 (2023), 34–39.

Before this radical revision of it, "Baptizing and Prophesying: Good and Evil in *The Violent Bear It Away*," was published as "Flannery O'Connor—*The Violent Bear It Away*," in *Finding a Common Thread: Understanding Great Texts from Homer to Flannery O'Connor*, ed. Robert C. Roberts, Scott Moore, and Donald D. Schmeltekopf (South Bend, Ind.: St. Augustine's Press, 2013), 305–22, 345–46.

A longer version of "Flannery O'Connor and Elizabeth Hester: A Friendship in Sacramental Suffering" was published in *Modern Theology* 24, no. 3 (2008): 387–411.

I am grateful to Farrar, Straus & Giroux for permission to quote from the following: Excerpts from *The Habit of Being: Letters of Flannery O'Connor*, edited by Sally Fitzgerald. Copyright © 1979 by Regina O'Connor. Excerpts from *Mystery and Manners* by Flannery O'Connor, Copyright © 1969 by the Estate of Mary Flannery O'Connor. Excerpts from *Flannery O'Connor: A Prayer Journal*. Copyright © 2013 by the Mary Flannery O'Connor Charitable Trust.